The Gallant Grouse

All About the Hunting and Natural History of Old Ruff

CECIL E. HEACOX

Illustrations by Wayne Trimm

David McKay Company, Inc.
NEW YORK

The author and publisher are deeply grateful to *Outdoor Life* Magazine for its courtesy in permitting the use of material originally published in different form in "The Grouse and I" (January 1969).

Library of Congress Cataloging in Publication Data

Heacox, Cecil E
    The gallant grouse.

    Bibliography: p.
    Includes index.
    1. Grouse shooting. 2. Ruffed grouse.
I. Title.
SK325.G7H4   799.2'48'61   79-22026
ISBN 0-679-51052-4

Book Design: Linda Readerman

3 4 5 6 7 8 9 10

MANUFACTURED IN THE UNITED STATES OF AMERICA

To the
New York State Ruffed Grouse Investigation
—and to its pioneering staff—
for the historical part it played in the
enduring saga of the gallant grouse.

Contents

THE GALLANT GROUSE

1

Opening Shot

Suddenly a ruffed grouse flushed from a juniper bush in a typical explosive lift-off. A handsome brown bird, the early morning
light catching the spread of its great fan, marked by a striking,
black band.

Caught up in the excitement of opening day, I shot too soon.
Two rapid-fire salvos saluted the first grouse of the season,
claiming only a few fluttering leaves.

Standing there with empty gun, I watched the grouse fly

straight ahead, suddenly sideslip behind a clump of birches, and reappear a moment later. Then, in a slanting dive, the bird quickly faded behind a shield of cedars and disappeared into the deep woods.

I sat down on a stone wall to savor the drama this great gamebird brings to the sport of wingshooting. Success had not marked my first shot of the season. But grouse hunting—fusing the exciting and the scenic—offers so many delights that a miss does not spoil the hunt.

Splendor surrounded me. A few tendrils of silver mist curled up from the Harlem Valley, dissolving into the brilliant blue sky. A bright sun burnished the golds and scarlets that October brushes across these foothills of the Taconics.

I thought about the delights of encountering the bird itself. A bird to seduce the eye and stir the spirit. An elegant bird with its imposing ruff and magnificent tail. A bold bird whose flamboyant flush expresses its ebullient personality. A grouse always greets a gunner with gusto.

The grouse is a challenging quarry with a boisterous, unnerving takeoff, followed by a powerful flight. Often the bird gets out of range before the gunner can line it up. And its never-ending repertoire of ruses: the frustrating trick of putting a tree between it and the hunter in an instant; the uncanny stratagem of flushing just when the hunter is in the thickest cover; the disconcerting tactic of changing course at the exact moment the gunner pulls the trigger. A commanding adversary inspiring the admiration and respect of every true grouse hunter.

As I sat there on the stone wall, I felt I could understand why the ruffed grouse appeals to others besides the hunter. A bird fascinating to the naturalist, intriguing to the ornithologist, and capturing the imagination of the bird watcher and so many others who are attracted to the world of nature.

A native gamebird whose lineage has been traced back to the Ice Age. An intrepid bird ranging over almost half of the North American continent. So resistant is it to civilization's increasing encroachments that it is established in the woodlands of 34 states—including Alaska and all the provinces and territories of Canada—and provides an annual bag of about six million birds. This yield varies with the ups and downs of the mysterious "grouse cycle."

A swashbuckling suitor whose woodland drumming booms through the coverts in a courtship ritual unique to the grouse. A solicitous mother who feigns a broken wing to divert attention from her chicks.

A hardy bird, able to survive the toughest winter: roosting in thick evergreens, diving under the snow to outlast a blizzard in a snug escape shelter, or feeding on tree buds and catkins—its distinctive habit of "budding"—when the ground is mantled with snow.

The ruffed grouse can generally survive the toughest winter.

So wedded to its wild ways is the ruffed grouse that it has stoutly resisted man's efforts to raise it by artificial methods since colonial times. The grouse responds best to management of its natural environment, as befits this most natural of creatures.

But the compelling call of the chase interrupted my thoughts. I got up from my stonewall philosopher's bench. It was time to get on with the hunt, time to renew acquaintance with the coverts. Time to climb ridges and slog through swamps, time to be thrilled once again by the electrifying moment of the flush, time to watch the forceful flight, time to suffer the disappointments of defeat and relish the elation of success.

But, above all, it was time to confront that most gallant of gamebirds, whose élan vital gives ruffed-grouse hunting a heartbeat all its own.

2
Ruffed-Grouse Roots

At least 25,000 years ago, the ruffed grouse was a well-established resident of North America. Although most of its contemporary species are long extinct, including the large and powerful dinosaurs and sabre-toothed tiger, *Bonasa umbellus* is still a thriving native gamebird found only on this continent.

Earlier in this century, a group of scientists digging in the Frankstown Cave near Altoona, Pennsylvania, uncovered bones of the ruffed grouse. The bones were later identified from a fragment of the cranium and a leg bone—the tibio-tarsus—by Dr. Alexander Wetmore,[44]* long associated with the National Museum of Natural History, Smithsonian Institution, and known to scientists as the dean of American ornithology.

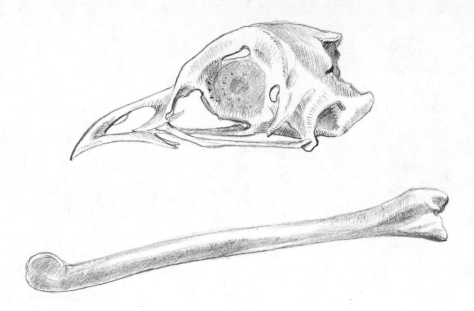

Bone fragments found in deposits of the Pleistocene Epoch indicate the ruffed grouse inhabited North America 25,000 years ago.

Across the Pennsylvania border in Maryland, railroad workers digging in a limestone spur near Corriganville broke through the roof of the Cumberland Cave. Again, Dr. Wetmore[45] identified the remains of more than forty species of animals—many now extinct. And, again, confirmed by the humerus bone of a left wing, the ruffed grouse, that hardy holdover, turned up.

Other ruffed-grouse bones have been found in scattered lo-

*Superior figures, here and in other citations throughout the text, refer to corresponding numbers that designate books and scientific articles listed in the Bibliography section, page 172.

cations: in the fissure beds of Arkansas, in Tennessee, and across the country in Potter Creek Cave, California.

All of these finds came from deposits of the Pleistocene Epoch: proof of the ruffed grouse's existence on this continent 250 centuries ago. Since the Pleistocene was characterized by widespread glacial ice, the evidence dramatically points up the strong survival instinct of the ruffed grouse.

Dr. Wetmore,[46] a world authority on fossil birds, places the advent of birds in the Jurassic age, about 125 million years ago. It strikes me that the earliest birdlike creature, Archaeopteryx, bears more than a faint resemblance to the ruffed grouse. Perhaps the roots of the ruffed grouse are even more deeply planted in geologic history.

Bone remains of ruffed grouse have also been found at Indian camping grounds over a large part of North America. These campsite digs show that the ruffed grouse was an important food item for the Indian.

Perhaps the first white man to see a ruffed grouse was Leif Ericson when he discovered the legendary Vineland around the year 1000 A.D.

Jacques Cartier encountered the bird, recording it in his journal in 1535. And probably he feasted on grouse during his

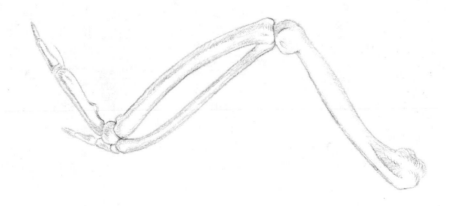

How the bones fit together in the wing of a ruffed grouse.

three explorations of the St. Lawrence Valley between 1534 and 1542.

The St. Lawrence Valley is still a stronghold of the bird nearly 500 years later—another tribute to the hardiness of the grouse. Surviving winter blizzards and summer heat waves, miraculously outmaneuvering torrential floods and raging forest

The author thinks that the ruffed grouse (left) bears more than a slight resemblance to the ancient Archaeopteryx (right).

fires, the ruffed grouse truly deserves the title, "King of American Gamebirds."

Although the geologic origin of the ruffed grouse is measured in epochs, its origin as a gamebird dates back less than 200 years.

In their highest flights of fancy, the New England settlers could hardly have foreseen that the grouse, abundant and unafraid of man, would become the most esteemed gamebird on the North American continent. To the early colonists, the bird was simply a staple table item, its delicious white meat a welcome change from the omnipresent salted cod.

As early as 1703, Baron de Lahontan[27] in his *New Voyages to America* noted the innocence of what he called the wood hen: "They sat in the trees and were killed one after another without offering to stir."

Before they became so sophisticated, ruffed grouse were fairly easy to kill or snare.

Potting birds with a fowling piece seemed a waste of powder and shot. Various methods of snaring were invented for capturing the bird on the ground and in trees. For tree-snatching, a wire loop on a long pole—also used for snaring fish—did the job. Whatever the method, whole flocks could be decimated in a short time, providing food for a long time.

Colonists who migrated from farms to villages and cities took their taste for the bird with them. But now they depended on those who still lived off the land for their supply.

Market hunting for grouse became a thriving business. It was as natural to go to the butcher for birds as it was for beef.

In 1820, New England pa'tridge, as the bird was and is called there, sold for 25 cents a brace. A good price in those days—enough to make market hunting a paying proposition. There is a record of a Taunton market hunter who sent about 1000 birds to nearby Boston, year after year.

Under the increasing gunning pressure of the market hunters, the ruffed grouse became wilder and warier. As word got around about this exciting new feathered target, a new breed of gunner evolved, marked by a special enthusiastic dedication.

But a gamebird really comes into its own when it becomes part of sporting literature. The ruffed grouse was honored early in American sporting history. In 1783, *The Sportsman's Companion, or an Essay on Shooting By a Gentleman*[5] was published in New York City. This volume was the first sporting book printed in the New World, making it a significant bit of Americana in addition to having the distinction of being the first to mention the grouse and grouse hunting.

In 1827, another anonymous volume appeared, *The American Shooters Manual by a Gentleman of Philadelphia County,*[4] the first comprehensive treatise on American field shooting.

The author sounded a keynote that rings as true today as the time the words were written:

"Grouse shooting may be justly considered the *ne plus ultra* of shooting, requiring more laborious sportsmen, better shots and better dogs, than any other sport in the shooting line in this country."

Yet it was more than a century later that the first book devoted exclusively to the ruffed grouse was published. The pivotal year was 1935.

Burton L. Spiller's *Grouse Feathers*[40] soon became a classic. And Spiller pointed the way for other prose laureates who blazed new trails to the ruffed-grouse coverts.

The ruffed grouse is a classic example of our rich heritage of natural resources. It's a rugged bird with the independent spirit only the outdoors of America could forge: a gamebird with an impressive past, securely locked into the present, and destined—it seems—for a resolute future.

3

Ruffed-Grouse Range

The king of gamebirds has a kingdom larger than any other American gamebird's. Not only is the ruffed grouse widely distributed but it also has well-established roots. An enduring bird in the face of a changing environment.

Geographically, the ruffed grouse is identified exclusively with the United States and Canada. Perhaps irrevocably so. The very first effort—possibly the only one—to introduce the ruffed grouse to Europe failed. Around 1672, Nicholas Denys,[16] repre-

sentative of France in Nova Scotia, twice tried to transport birds across the Atlantic in the slow sailing ships of the day.

"But when approaching France," he reported, "they die, which has made me believe that our air must be contrary to their good."

The vast range of the ruffed grouse stretches across the waistband of North America, from the Atlantic to the Pacific. It's a territory that covers large sections of the United States and Canada, extending through more than 30° of latitude—about one-third of the continent.

The eastern realm of the ruffed grouse extends from the conifers of Labrador to the woodlots of New England; along the eastern seaboard states to the laurels of northern Georgia; from the territories and prairie provinces of Canada down through the Midwest states and Appalachia. Its western domain stretches from the woodlands of the Yukon, Porcupine, and lesser known rivers of Alaska, through British Columbia to northwestern California, dipping into Idaho, Utah, Montana, and Wyoming.

The bird's range has been nibbled away on the fringes of the Deep South. As far back as 1831, John James Audubon[6] observed large numbers of grouse along the Mississippi River in Tennessee. Across the boundary in Mississippi, grouse populations rapidly became scarcer and he noted: "As you approach the City of Natchez, they disappear."

And today, the ruffed grouse has completely disappeared from the Mississippi scene. Nor is it a resident of Alabama, Mississippi's neighbor on the east. In a report from Alabama: "Records indicate that the ruffed grouse was present in the mountains of North Alabama but had completely disappeared by the early 1900s."

The northern edge of the bird's range is probably much the same as it was at the end of the last Ice Age. With more certainty, the same as in 1860, when naturalist Bernard Ross[37] recorded the species at Lapierre House in the Mackenzie Basin of the Yukon Territory.

In the continental distribution pattern, however, population densities are far from uniform. The pattern has many holes and some very large, as in much of the Great Plains. Small gaps often show up within the best parts of the bird's range. One such example is New England, with its high concentration of population and industry, where man's hand on the land has irretrievably destroyed so much of what was once ideal habitat.

Nature, too, influences distribution patterns. Topography, climate, vegetation, and dozens of knowns (and perhaps unknowns) tip the ecological scales that determine the suitability of a ruffed grouse's environmental niche.

Even the physical capabilities of the ruffed grouse itself sometimes determine range pattern. Such as, the flight limits of the bird.

For example, the mainland of Newfoundland always had a resident population of ruffed grouse. But on the island part of the province, in the Gulf of St. Lawrence, 45 miles from the nearest grouse habitat, the bird was not native. However, it has been successfully introduced.

Yet, the ruffed grouse is established on Prince Edward Island, also in the Gulf of St. Lawrence, requiring a flight of only 10 miles. On Isle Royale in Lake Superior, 15 miles from Michigan's mainland, the bird is absent.

These examples might be only circumstantial evidence suggesting that the maximum flight limit of the ruffed grouse is between 10 and 15 miles.

Walter L. Palmer,[34] however, after testing the flight capabilities of the bird over water in Michigan, concluded that ruffed grouse could not negotiate even a 1-mile expanse.

Possibly ruffed grouse reached distant islands during winter freeze-ups, making the journey in short hops over ice floes.

In various sections of its range, the ruffed grouse seems to inspire a strong interest in reestablishing the bird.

Alabama tried to reintroduce the ruffed grouse several years ago. Experimental releases were made in several areas of its former range with little or no success in reestablishing a population. An occasional sighting of a grouse has been reported in Alabama, but it has not been possible to develop a huntable population.

Delaware, Illinois, Missouri, and Arkansas have investigations underway to determine the feasibility of bringing back the bird.

Delaware reports that the last recorded instance of a grouse being taken by a hunter was in the early 1800s. In the 1960s, a number of wild-caught grouse from Pennsylvania were acquired to evaluate their Delaware survival potential. Later additional birds were brought in from Massachusetts and Maine.

The data indicate that grouse may be able to survive marginally in Delaware but are unsuited for establishing a self-sustaining population sizable enough to provide hunting.

Illinois made a release of ruffed grouse from Ohio in 1967 and from Indiana in 1972. Stocked birds have been spotted considerable distances from the release sites. But since the releases were small, it will probably take time to determine whether open hunting seasons are possible.

A more encouraging report comes from Missouri: "The ruffed grouse *(Bonasa umbellus)* was almost extirpated in Missouri by the turn of the century. Hunting seasons on grouse were closed in 1905. . . . The elimination of grouse in Missouri was probably caused by destruction of habitat. . . . Improved habitat conditions resulting from fire protection and the elimination of free range grazing offered an opportunity to reestablish grouse in Missouri. Wild-trapped grouse from Ohio, Indiana, Iowa, Kentucky, Minnesota, and Wisconsin have been released on six areas in the state. . . . and reestablished. . . . on three of the six release sites. . . . grouse now occupy approximately 100 square miles in at least 10 counties."

Another optimistic note is the outlook for ruffed grouse in Arkansas. The Game and Fish Commission is very much interested in restoring the grouse. Previous restoration efforts failed, and now a source of wild-trapped grouse is being sought. Missouri, Arkansas' neighbor, has been successful in restocking ruffed grouse, and Arkansas is confident of being able to restore grouse to much of its prior range.

Even though the ruffed grouse may play only a cameo role in these states and grouse gunning may not be in the hunting picture, it is heartwarming to people who love the bird that in the spring, its drum roll may again echo through the woodlands.

The primary goal of reestablishment programs, however, is the restoration of grouse hunting. Successful projects in Indiana, Iowa, and Nevada are examples.

Following the pattern in neighboring states, Indiana's grouse population experienced a decline. In 1937, hunting seasons were discontinued.

A reintroduction program began in 1961, using wild-trapped native birds from Indiana's Brown County State Park. The success of the project permitted, in 1965, the first modern-day hunting in seven counties. Reestablishment has been extended to eleven other counties, where open hunting seasons on ruffed grouse are expected in the future.

In Iowa, the ruffed grouse was so abundant a native that a daily limit of 25 birds was allowed when the first bag limits were put on grouse in 1878. A steady decline of ruffed grouse continued into the twentieth century, and hunting seasons on the bird were abolished in 1923.

Although attempts have been made to reintroduce the bird into state forests in southern parts of Iowa, that state's experience is a fine example of the ruffed grouse's ability to hold on, even in marginal habitat such as a section in the northeastern part of the state along the Mississippi River. Here the grouse made a comeback on its own, and the area was reopened for a 16-day hunting season in 1968. The 1100 hunters who enjoyed the first ruffed-grouse hunting season in 45 years bagged 720 birds.

Since then, the special quality that the ruffed grouse gives to bird hunting sparked a growing interest in grouse hunting in Iowa. The result is that in 1977, some 3000 hunters harvested about 10,000 birds.

According to an old distribution map, ruffed grouse were

native to only a small northeastern section of Nevada. But the birds were too scarce to provide hunting.

In 1963, wild-trapped birds from Idaho were released in the Soldier Creek section of the Ruby Mountains. That may have been the first time an airplane played a role in such an operation. The birds were picked up in Pocatello, Idaho, by plane and flown to Elko, Nevada. Then they were whisked by truck to the release site. Less than four hours elapsed from the time the birds were picked up at Pocatello until they were released in the Rubys.

The introduction was successful, and a hunting season opened in 1970. Nevada notes: "The ruffed grouse population does seem to be expanding in the Ruby Mountains. However, the harvest is so limited that we do not have a good reading on what the total number of birds taken per year would be. . . . One of the primary problems is the fact that they occupy very dense, vegetative groves found in canyon bottoms and hunters simply have not found a technique for hunting them. (We are) sure that as time goes by we will find a cult of ruffed grouse hunters keying in on the Ruby Mountains area."

In these days, when all wildlife is caught in a squeeze between an expanding population and a contracting environment, reestablishing grouse hunting is a major accomplishment. But to enlarge the bird's range by introducing ruffed grouse to areas where it was not native originally—and produce huntable populations—is a landmark achievement.

Michigan has done just that, first successfully introducing wild-trapped birds—some stock came from Wisconsin—on Beaver Island in Lake Michigan and Bois Blanc Island and Drummond Island in Lake Huron.

Richard J. Moran and Walter L. Palmer,[32] commenting on the first experiment: "The progeny of these 200 birds have been hunted annually since 1954, with a total combined harvest of at least 8000 birds—a profitable return on a small initial investment."

Later, wild-trapped ruffed grouse were successfully established on High Island and Garden Island in Lake Michigan.

Canada, too, has a showcase example of ruffed-grouse range expansion. Although the ruffed grouse was a resident of the Labrador part of Newfoundland from the beginning, the bird was not native to the island part of that province.

In 1956, wild-trapped birds from Nova Scotia, Maine, and Wisconsin were released on the island part of Newfoundland. The population has prospered and shows a steady increase. For example, during the 1973–74 hunting season, hunters bagged 6000 ruffed grouse; the 1976–77 season produced 29,000.

Newfoundland's Wildlife Division states: "The latest kill figures show that the Ruffed Grouse"—I like their capital-letter distinction—"has adapted well to the Newfoundland environment since their introduction."

On the Province of Quebec's Anticosti Island in the Gulf of St. Lawrence, the ruffed grouse was not a native bird. In 1911, birds from Quebec's mainland were successfully introduced by Henri Meunier, then the owner of the island. Anticosti Island provides good grouse gunning today.

All these efforts to introduce and reintroduce the bird are bench marks—possibly historic ones—in maintaining, restoring, and even extending the range of that remarkably durable native, the ruffed grouse.

In reviewing the history of these ruffed-grouse projects, I am impressed by the generosity of wildlife agencies in donating wild-trapped birds. As a retired member of the New York State Conservation Department, I find it gratifying that the old brotherhood spirit still prevails.

And the continuing freemasonry of the conservation clan sometimes promotes backscratching transactions. In the Newfoundland-Maine exchange, for instance, Wayne Trimm, this book's artist, tells us that Newfoundland caribou were traded for Maine grouse.

Maps are a graphic but abstract way of showing the range of the ruffed grouse. Tallies of the states and provinces are more concrete indicators of the bird's range and abundance.

Thirty-four states and the ten provinces and two territories of Canada have open hunting seasons on ruffed grouse.

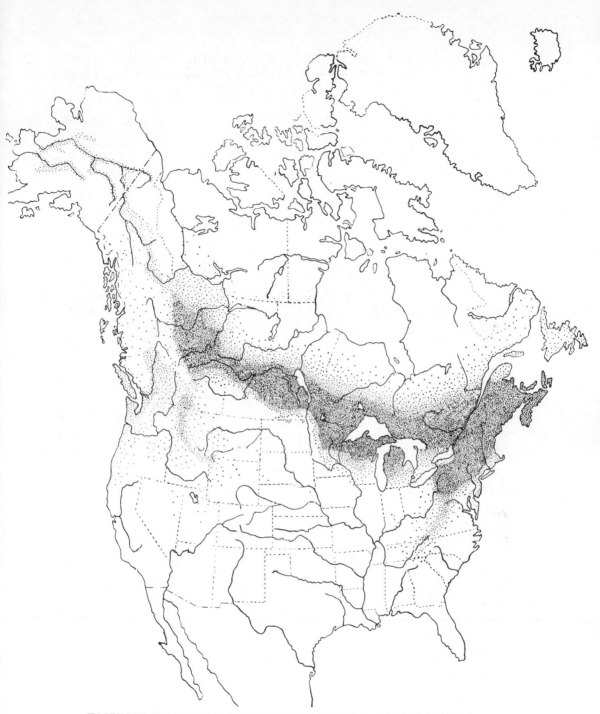

RUFFED-GROUSE DISTRIBUTION IN U.S. AND CANADA

ADAPTED FROM DISTRIBUTION MAP IN The Ruffed Grouse *BY GARDINER BUMP, ROBERT W. DARROW, FRANK C. EDMINSTER, WALTER CRISSEY. COURTESY NEW YORK STATE DEPARTMENT OF ENVIRONMENTAL CONSERVATION.*

RUFFED-GROUSE HUNTING SEASONS
UNITED STATES

State	Season	State	Season
Alabama		Montana	x
Alaska	x	Nebraska	
Arizona		Nevada	x
Arkansas	*	New Hampshire	x
California	x	New Jersey	x
Colorado		New Mexico	
Connecticut	x	New York	x
Delaware	*	North Carolina	x
Florida		North Dakota	x
Georgia	x	Ohio	x
Hawaii		Oklahoma	
Idaho	x	Oregon	x
Illinois	*	Pennsylvania	x
Indiana	x	Rhode Island	x
Iowa	x	South Carolina	x
Kansas		South Dakota	x
Kentucky	x	Tennessee	x
Louisiana		Texas	
Maine	x	Utah	x
Maryland	x	Vermont	x
Massachusetts	x	Virginia	x
Michigan	x	Washington	x
Minnesota	x	West Virginia	x
Mississippi		Wisconsin	x
Missouri	*	Wyoming	x

x   Open hunting season on ruffed grouse
*   Reintroduction experiment in progress

Getting reliable estimates on annual harvests is a goal that has eluded wildlife biologists since the beginning of modern game management. Satisfactory methods are yet to be developed. Some of the methods that have been tried and found wanting are mail questionnaires, license-stub returns, field checks, and telephone checks.

My own experience in state government with sportsmen's reports has led me to believe that hunters and fishermen can be placed into three categories: (1) those who provide the McCoy; (2) those who are reluctant to reveal their success and therefore shave their figures; and (3) those who are not so successful but also are reluctant to admit the truth and therefore beef-up their figures.

In spite of the many drawbacks in trying to estimate game harvests, the biologist tries to arrive at a fairly realistic appraisal so the administrator can formulate policy. As a note, included with New Brunswick statistics, states: "They are ball-park figures, which I feel are sufficiently reliable to allow management decisions."

In any attempt to present a continent-wide picture of the ruffed-grouse harvest, the "grouse cycle" becomes a troublesome factor. The lows and highs of the cycle occur at different times in different parts of its range. In Canada, for example, both Manitoba (35,500 birds) and Saskatchewan (12,700 birds) were in the low stage of the cycle in 1973. Yet the same year, Ontario (1,233,000) was in a peak period.

Sometimes, regardless of the cycle's stage, other factors intrude, frequently causing crash declines in a particular section. Prince Edward Island, for instance, had a fine grouse harvest in 1976: some 16,800 birds. But in the very next year, the bag dropped to 9290. The biologist's explanation: "The 1976 season was a reflection of favorable hatching conditions while the 1977 decline can be attributed to a cold, wet hatching season."

Regardless of cyclic and seasonal weather variations, the annual range-wide harvest seems to balance out and runs into the impressive figure of about 6,000,000 ruffed grouse.

HUNTERS' HARVEST * RUFFED GROUSE * UNITED STATES

State	Annual Hunters' Take	Season
Alaska*	*	
California	900	1977
Connecticut	29,000	Recent average
Georgia*	*	
Idaho	93,700	1977
Indiana	450–950	Recent spread
Iowa	10,000	1977
Kentucky	41,000	1977–78
Maine	88,471	1976
Maryland	11,559	1974–75
Massachusetts	38,672	1976
Michigan	728,500	1976
Minnesota	630,000	1977
Montana	54,700	1977
Nevada*	*	
New Hampshire	50,000–115,000	Recent spread
New Jersey	49,105	1976–77
New York	150,000	Recent average
North Carolina	30,000	Recent average
North Dakota	500–5,000	Recent spread
Ohio	131,000	1975
Oregon	29,590	1977
Pennsylvania	268,000	Recent average

Rhode Island	2,000–5,000	Recent spread
South Carolina	110	1966
South Dakota	500	Recent average
Tennessee	30,080	1977–78
Utah	24,561	1974
Vermont	75,000	Recent average
Virginia	112,032	1975–76
Washington	207,450	Recent average
West Virginia	158,400	1975–76
Wisconsin	500,000	Recent average
Wyoming	6,616	1975
Total**	3,551,896	

*   Alaska is in the process of developing a method for monitoring the ruffed-grouse harvest; Georgia does not collect harvest data on minor species; Nevada has so recently reintroduced ruffed grouse and the take is so limited, it has not been possible to get a good reading on hunters' take.

**   Where a state reports a spread, its lowest figure is used in calculating total.

In the middle 1970s, ruffed-grouse hunting action on the North American continent shaped up by region like this:

In New England (Maine, New Hampshire, Vermont, Massachusetts, Rhode Island, and Connecticut) where grouse hunting had its first flowering, the estimated annual take of ruffed grouse ran about 245,000. Maine topped the list with 88,000 birds.

The Middle Atlantic states (New York, New Jersey, and Pennsylvania) had sizable populations of not only *Homo sapiens* but also *Bonasa umbellus*. For the region, the total bag was a surprising 467,000 birds, with Pennsylvania providing 268,000.

The five seaboard states to the south (Maryland, Virginia, North Carolina, South Carolina, and Georgia) had a total harvest of 154,000 grouse, Virginia leading with a take of 112,000.

Ohio and the heartland of Appalachia (West Virginia, Kentucky, and Tennessee) added about 360,000 to the United States take.

The upper Midwest (Michigan, Minnesota, and Wisconsin) held the richest lode of ruffed grouse, demonstrated by an amazing bag of well over 1,500,000 birds.

As in the Deep South and the arid Southwest, the ruffed grouse is missing in most of the Middle West farm states. Yet

HUNTERS' HARVEST * RUFFED GROUSE * CANADA

Province or Territory	Annual Hunters' Take	Season
Alberta	300,000	1977
British Columbia	186,000	1976
Manitoba	75,500	1975
New Brunswick	295,000	1977
Newfoundland	29,000	1976–77
Nova Scotia	113,509	1977
Ontario	1,359,100	1975–76
Prince Edward Island	9,290	1977
Quebec*		
Saskatchewan	74,210	1977
Northwest Territories	5,743	1975–76
Yukon Territory	5,570	1976
Total	2,452,922	

* Quebec combines all small-game species into one group.

North Dakota and South Dakota, chiefly in the Black Hills, have enough birds to warrant an open hunting season, combining to provide a modest annual bag varying from 1000 to 5000.

The ruffed grouse is not present in the heart of the Rocky Mountains—Colorado. However, the adjoining states—Wyoming and Utah—and Montana and Idaho add another 179,000 birds to the annual bag.

The aggregate bag in the Pacific Coast states (California, Oregon, Washington, and Alaska) was estimated at 238,000 grouse, with Washington providing a top-heavy 207,000.

The Dominion of Canada is a treasury of ruffed grouse, the most important upland gamebird in most of its vast area.

Newfoundland and the Maritimes (New Brunswick, Nova Scotia, and Prince Edward Island) yielded an annual harvest of 447,000 birds during the middle of the 1970s.

Quebec and Ontario together came in with a bag of about 2,000,000 birds.

The Prairie Provinces (Manitoba, Saskatchewan, and Alberta) swell the game bag by 449,000 birds, with Alberta contributing a whopping 300,000. An Alberta biologist comments: "Even with 52,000 hunters taking 300,000 birds per year, ruffed grouse remain unharvested over a large percentage of their range in Alberta."

British Columbia is another prolific ruffed-grouse province, with a harvest of 186,000 birds. British Columbia's Fish and Wildlife Branch notes: "The ruffed-grouse population in this province is estimated to be 4,000,000 and increasing."

The Northwest Territories and Yukon Territory each contribute about 5000 birds to Canada's ruffed-grouse game bag. And, there's a population boom in the Yukon. The government ornithologist says: "Since 1975, the density of ruffed grouse in the Yukon has been increasing dramatically. Concurrently, the harvest has been going up."

Abundant and widely distributed, the ruffed grouse not only holds on firmly to its territory—even expanding its frontiers—but also has retained a firm hold on the hearts of hunters. Another echo of its greatness.

4

An Outside Look at the Ruffed Grouse

A handsome bird, the ruffed grouse, its mantle of feathers a mottled motif of mellow grays or rich browns. With its dark-banded tail at full fan, its imperial crest erect, and its iridescent, regal ruff extended, it is more imposing and majestic than any other gamebird.

When a ruffed grouse is lined up over a gun barrel, 30 yards out and zooming away at top speed, it seems to be a duplicate of every other grouse on the wing. But as a bird hunter quickly learns, the ruffed grouse comes in two basic color phases — gray and brown. In many parts of its range, the brown phase has a decidedly reddish cast.

In each color phase, the bird's plumage seduces the eye. In America, the ruffed grouse was first honored on canvas in 1810 with a life-size portrait by Alexander Wilson, the Scottish bird watcher who became "the father of American ornithology." Audubon, his great rival, followed in 1824 with a painting that, for the first time, portrayed the bird in a natural setting. Later, the prints of Nathaniel Currier and James Merritt Ives, depictors of early Americana, made the bird a familiar subject in the home-spun art of the day. And the picturesque ruffed grouse has been inspiring wildlife artists ever since.

Although the ruffed grouse has the spirit of a fighting cock, it is only about the size of a bantam rooster. For the best available data on the measurements of the ruffed grouse, I rely on Frank C. Edminster[18,19], my teacher in Game Management at Cornell. Eddy wrote *The Ruffed Grouse* and *American Game Birds of Field and Forest.* He was also one of the four leading researchers on the New York State Ruffed Grouse Investigation. That 13-year study was wrapped up in *The Ruffed Grouse — Life History — Propagation — Management* by Gardiner Bump, Frank C. Edminster, Robert W. Darrow, and Walter F. Crissey.[10] A monumental volume

The average adult male ruffed grouse is slightly heavier than the average adult female ruffed grouse.

of nearly 1000 pages, weighing about the same as my Ithaca 20-gauge grouse gun.

In the course of the Investigation, Eddy measured hundreds of grouse—more than most hunters shoot in a lifetime. From tip of the bill to tip of the tail, lengths ranged from 15 to 20 inches, averaging out at 17 inches. Wingspread varied from 22 to 25 inches, the median around 23 inches.

With a target of that size, how is it possible to miss so often?

The weight of adult male ruffed grouse, in the fall, averages 1 pound, 7 ounces; females, 1 pound, 5 ounces. Ruffed grouse reach their heaviest weight in November and December. About the middle of January, weight loss begins. In March, a bird will have lost from 1¼ to 2½ ounces.

In New York, the heaviest grouse on record is a bird taken at the century's turn in the Adirondack Mountains which scaled 2 pounds, 4 ounces—shot and weighed by John Burnham, Chief of Fish and Game, New York State Conservation Department.

New York State's heavyweight champion of ruffed grouse came from the Adirondack Mountains.

Although grouse weights are fairly uniform, each bird is an individual in plumage pattern and color. These differences do not show up when a bird is taken only here and there or now and then. But when a number of birds are in hand at the same time, the differences become strikingly apparent.

Such luck does not favor a grouse hunter often. But I recall a memorable day of gunning with Victor Coty—grouse hunter, dry-fly fisherman, photographer, lecturer—on a hunt circling Lake of the Woods on the western flank of the Adirondacks. The birds were at the peak of a cycle. And with the help of Queen, Victor's blue belton English setter, we both bagged our limit.

At the end of the day, when we laid out the grouse to pluck, it was obvious that five were gray-phase birds and three were brown.

Taking a break from plucking, we looked more closely at the feathers spread around us. A great variety of pattern differences showed up in the arrangement and size of spots and bars and varying shades of color in both brown and gray birds.

"Just like our fingerprints," Victor suggested. "No two are alike."

As they say, a bird is known by its feathers and a ruffed grouse, as our sore fingers attested that day, has several thousand. I never had the patience to count them. But Dr. John E. Trainer, an ambitious fellow student when I was taking conservation courses at Cornell, did just that. He found the number to be 4342, amounting to about 7 percent of the bird's total weight.

And the ruffed grouse can fluff up these thousands of feathers, making itself seem to double in size and providing a

When the ruffed grouse fluffs up its thousands of feathers, it seems to double in size.

natural insulation on winter days. The dark feathers convert the rays from even a faint winter sun into solar heat.

Although there are many individual differences in appearance, the ruffed grouse is always an elegant bird, from head to tail.

Crowning the head is a crest, which rises when the bird is excited. That happens when, for instance, you encounter a mother grouse protecting her brood.

Especially striking is the eye of a grouse, with that same yellow cast that gives the wild gleam to the eyes of hawks and eagles.

The grouse's majestic ruff—feather tracts on each side of the neck—is a centerpiece attraction. This adornment gives the species its name and is a distinction that sets it apart from other members of the gamebird galaxy.

More prominent in the male, the ruff is occasionally reddish-brown but mostly is made up of broad, black feathers that are square on the outer edge and have a purplish or greenish metallic luster.

Lying beneath each tract of ruff feathers is a specialized muscle that enables the grouse to fluff its ruff at will. This phenomenon is especially spectacular when the male is in a romantic mood.

The legs of most gamebirds are bare, but the tarsus of the ruffed grouse is feathered about halfway down to the feet. Unlike a gamecock or a pheasant, a grouse has no spur on its leg. But beginning in the late fall, fringelike appendages, derived from the skin, grow along the sides of the toes and form "snow-shoes"—an external adjunct that makes it easier to travel in deep snow. These snowshoes are a distinguishing grouse characteristic and are part of the bird's survival equipment in northern winters.

But the most striking feature of the ruffed grouse is its magnificent tail. The grouse's tail can be spread, raised, or lowered according to the bird's mood. No other gamebird has such a tail. A neighbor aptly calls this bird the "fan-tailed partridge."

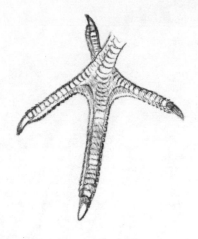

In summer, the ruffed grouse's foot looks trim.

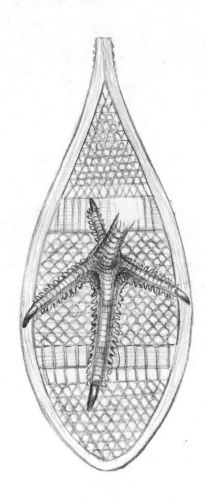

Beginning in late fall, fringelike appendages grow along the sides of the ruffed grouse's toes.

A masterpiece of nature's handiwork, the tail of the ruffed grouse was at one time used in an unusual example of human handiwork. In 1672, Nicholas Denys[16] reported that grouse tails were shipped from Nova Scotia to France where they were made into hand fans, veritable works of art, coveted by ladies of high fashion in the court of Louis XIV.

And in America, grouse feathers make up some part of the flies used in wet-fly fishing. Patterns such as March Brown, Olive Wren, McKenzie, and, of course, the Partridge.

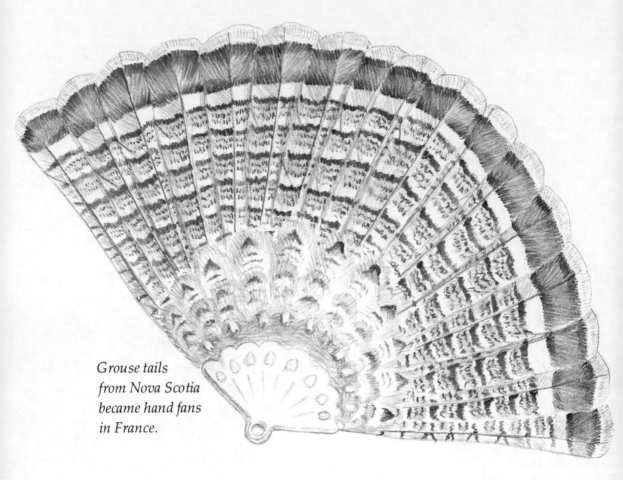

*Grouse tails
from Nova Scotia
became hand fans
in France.*

Normally a ruffed grouse's tail has a complement of 18 feathers, but tails varying from 16 to 20 feathers have been recorded. Each tail feather has 6 to 11 narrow, wavy, blackish bars and a wide band near the end of the feather, set off by grayish-white bars on either side. In gray-phase birds, the band is invariably black; in brown-phase birds, the band is frequently black and sometimes reddish.

This band is more than just decorative; it is a key to deter-

The Partridge wet-fly pattern.

The March Brown wet-fly pattern.

mining the sex of the ruffed grouse. Positive determination of
sex, of course, can be confirmed only by dissection to examine
the sex organs. But for most of us, not bound by the strict pa-
rameters of science, a close look at the tail of a ruffed grouse will
usually reveal the bird's sex.

If the wide band across the tail is unbroken, the bird is almost always a male. During the 13-year New York State Ruffed
Grouse Investigation, only one female with a solid tail band was
recorded.

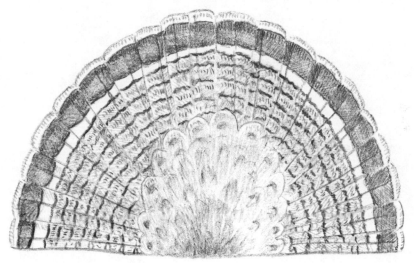

Tail of typical male ruffed grouse has unbroken dark band near outer edge.

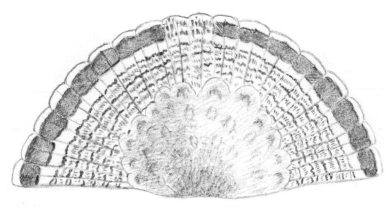

*Tail of typical female ruffed grouse has dark band "broken" at two middle
feathers.*

If the continuity of the band is broken at the two middle feathers, the bird is usually a female. However, some fully-developed adult males have tails with a hazy, or wholly interrupted break on the middle feathers. Because of this inconsistency, a better test, the New York State Ruffed Grouse Investigation was the first to discover, is the length of the tail. If the middle feathers are 6¼ inches or longer, the bird is certain to be a male; if 5¾ inches or shorter, it is almost always a female. For that "iffy" half inch from 5¾ to 6¼, examination of the sex organs is the only certain way.

Female   *Male*

At first glance, both sexes seem to have the same shape. But the cockbird's head is deeper from crown to chin and the neck is thicker. So he has a heavier and more rugged appearance than the daintier hen. The throat of the male joins the body directly under the eye; while the female's neckline is behind the eye, giving her that "plump as a partridge" perfect-36 outline.

Just as there are distinctions in appearance between the sexes, there are also differences, mostly in color, between whole grouse populations in the various sections of its extensive range.

What controls the color of the grouse's plumage is another mystery of this great gamebird.

In the range-wide picture, a strong case can be made for geography and climate as the chief influences that determine color variations in the plumage of the bird.

John W. Aldrich[1] of the Smithsonian Institution, the leading authority on American gamebird distribution, has put together some pieces in this intriguing puzzle. "In the ruffed grouse," he says, "we find a classic example of the correlation of intensity of coloration with the amount of moisture in the environment, as well as with the density and background shades of the vegetation cover, themselves correlated with moisture. Thus the darkest ruffed grouse are in the lush forests of the Olympic peninsula rain forest and the palest in the relatively arid aspen groves of the Great Basin mountains of Utah and the low hills rising out of the short-grass prairies of the central states and provinces."

Protective coloration seems to prevail in most of the bird's wide range. But this still doesn't solve the mystery of color variations between individual birds in your own favorite covert. Only last spring I spotted a brick-red grouse dusting on our hilltop road. It was the first of this color phase I've ever seen in my home covers.

Just as white-fleshed trout and pink-fleshed trout live in the same pool and eat the same foods, so gray-phase and brown-phase ruffed grouse share the same covert. The last two birds I bagged were shot not more than 50 yards apart on the same hunt. One was a beautiful gray-phase bird. The other was an even more beautiful brown-phase bird. The crops of both birds were stuffed with apple seeds from a nearby abandoned orchard.

Even more puzzling: gray-phase birds and brown-phase birds have been found in the same brood; to cloud the picture still more, it has been observed that some ruffed grouse raised in captivity incline toward the brown phase at the beginning of feathering but more toward the gray phase after several molts.

Because of variations in the ruffed grouse's appearance and its extensive geographic range, which includes so many different ethnic groups, it is understandable that the bird became known by so many different common names.

If it's true that the first inhabitants of the North American continent crossed the Bering Strait from Asia to Alaska, the Eskimos were the first natives to honor this bird with a name. The name comes out something like *kh-tuk.* Could it be that the name was derived from the staccato cluck of the grouse?

Much of the ruffed grouse's range coincided with lands occupied by Indians, and nearly every tribe had its own name for the bird.

In southern New England, the Pequots called the bird a *cut-quass;* to their neighbors, the Narragansetts, it was a *paupock;* to the Chippewas of the Lake Superior region, a *wen-gi-da-bi-ne.* In the Finger Lakes region of Central New York, where I shot my first grouse, the Oneidas of the Iroquois Nation gave it the name of *ohquase.*

In the French settlements of the early 1600s, the ruffed grouse was christened with a variety of names still in common usage: *coq de bruyère à fraise, grosse gélinotte du Canada,* and *perdrix des bois francs.* Today's hunting regulations of the Province of Quebec list the bird as *gélinotte huppée.*

In Pennsylvania Dutch country, the German influence was revealed in *fesond.* In the Quaker colony, the bird was called a pheasant, as it was south of the Mason-Dixon Line. Or mountain pheasant, a name still common in some sections.

In New England, the bird is a partridge, which in Down East dialect comes out "pa'tridge"; in Michigan, Minnesota, and Wisconsin, the name is apt to be shortened to "pat."

But the bird is not a pheasant nor is it a true partridge. It is classified scientifically as belonging to the grouse family.

Although local names die hard and there are still some regional holdouts, most of today's bird hunters have accepted "ruffed grouse" as the authentic common name—named in acknowledgment of the bird's distinctive feathered collar.

In the ornithologist's world, too, the ruffed grouse collected many scientific names. Just as it acquired so many common names because of the differences in plumage pattern and color, so were scientists led to consider each variation, at first, a separate species and later a subspecies.

The early settlers were too busy hewing out the wilderness to have much time for scientific observation of the natural world. And in England, the plants and animals sent back to the homeland by colonists stirred little interest.

But notable exceptions occurred in both England and America, exceptions marked by an especially fervent enthusiasm for the flora and fauna of the New World.

In America, John Bartram,[7] native-born Quaker farmer, was endowed with a compulsive passion for observing the wildflowers and the wildlife around his farm near Philadelphia.

Across the Atlantic, Robert Petre, wealthy young English lord, shared Bartram's enthusiasm for the plants and creatures of His Majesty's American colonies. With a highly developed acquisitive instinct and the pocketbook to support it, he sought help to enhance his garden and menagerie. Lord Petre went to his friend Peter Colinson for guidance. Colinson, a Quaker like Bartram, was in close touch with naturalists in the Pennsylvania colony.

In 1750, John Bartram sent Colinson a specimen of a bird representing one of the most unusual examples of American fauna—the bird now known as the ruffed grouse. Letters followed, describing the drumming behavior of the bird and the difficulty of raising it in captivity.

Colinson turned over Bartram's material to George Edwards,[20] British naturalist. Edwards' accounts of the bird, based on Bartram's information, were published as "On the Pheasant in Pennsylvania and the Otis Minor (1754)" and in "Gleanings of Natural History (1758)." The latter account was accompanied by a color plate labeled "Ruffed Heath-cock or

Grous," apparently painted in England with the Bartram specimen
as the model.

The 1758 paper by Edwards came to the attention of Carl
Linnaeus.[30] And the ruffed grouse was christened with a scien-
tific name for the first time in the 1766 edition of his *Systema
Naturae.*

Systema Naturae was the crowning point of Linnaeus' life-
long effort to bring logical order to the chaos existing in the classification of the world's plants and animals.

He worked out a system in which the classification of an
animal is structured like a tree: the trunk denoting family; limbs,
the genus; and twigs, the species. Linnaeus was probably the
first to realize that without the universal language of science, we
cannot be certain that other people will know what species we
are talking about.

Because of the similarity in appearance to the grouse of Europe, Linnaeus assigned the American bird to the grouse family,
Tetraonidae, and put the bird in the genus *Tetrao* and in the species *umbellus.* The "specific" name referred to the bird's magnificent umbrellalike ruff.

By this route, John Bartram's bird from Pennsylvania became the type specimen for the scientific classification of the bird
we now commonly call the ruffed grouse. It is very fitting, therefore, that the official bird of the Commonwealth of Pennsylvania
is the ruffed grouse.

In America, scientific classification burgeoned in the early
part of the nineteenth century, struggling to keep pace with the
astonishing number of animals and plants being discovered as
settlers pushed westward.

Explorers and naturalists believed they were discovering a
new species when they encountered a slightly different looking
ruffed grouse in other parts of the North American continent.

The Lewis and Clark Expedition (1804–06) named the dark,
rufous bird they discovered in the rain forests of the northwest,
Tetrao fusca. In 1833, David Douglas,[17] a Scottish botanist who
was traveling in America, encountered the same bird and named

it *Tetrao sabini,* noting the reddish shade as contrasted to the gray grouse of the Peace River region in Canada, which he had named *Tetrao umbelloides.*

In 1840, George Robert Gray,[24] British naturalist, decided that, although the ruffed grouse of the New World was in the same family as the Old World grouse, it was a different genus. He reclassified it as *Bonasa umbellus.* The Latin word for wild bull is *Bonasa.* Possibly Gray chose this name because of the similarity between the drumming sound of a grouse and the bellowing of a bull.

Gray's new generic name, *Bonasa,* put the bird in a classification by itself. To the hunter, the ruffed grouse has always been in a class by itself.

Bonasa umbellus, as a classification, has stood the test of time. But in view of so many regional color variations among ruffed grouse, the scientists have had a field day naming subspecies.

Finally the taxonomic dust has settled, and John W. Aldrich[1] gives an authoritative and comprehensive roundup of the accepted subspecies of *Bonasa umbellus* correlated with their habitats: ". . . the ruffed grouse occupies a relatively large number of life areas with which its racial variation seems to be rather well correlated. For example, the St. Lawrence ruffed grouse (*Bonasa umbellus togata*) lives chiefly in the northern hardwood-conifer area, the eastern ruffed grouse (*B. u. umbellus*) and the Appalachian ruffed grouse (*B. u. monticola*) in the eastern deciduous forest area; the midwestern ruffed grouse (*B. u. mediana*) in the oak-savannah woodlands; the gray ruffed grouse (*B. u. umbelloides*) in the closed boreal area; the Yukon ruffed grouse (*B. u. yukonensis*) in the open boreal area; the hoary ruffed grouse (*B. u. incana*) in the drier montane woodland and aspen parkland areas; the Vancouver ruffed grouse (*B. u. brunnescens*) and the Olympic ruffed grouse (*B. u. castanea*) in the wettest sections of the Pacific rain forest; the Pacific ruffed grouse (*B. u. sabini*) in a slightly drier phase of this same climax type; and the Idaho ruffed grouse *(B. u. phaia)* in the drier disjunct of this type, known as the Columbian forest, in northern Idaho and southeastern

British Columbia. The Columbian ruffed grouse (*B. u. affinis*) occupies the still drier habitats of the montane woodland area of interior British Columbia, Washington, and Oregon."

Despite the ruffed grouse's diversity of feathered garbs—guises that beget so many common and scientific names—there's one overriding characteristic that describes *Bonasa umbellus:* the ruffed grouse looks the way a gamebird should.

5

An Inside Look at the Ruffed Grouse

Although the outside of the ruffed grouse, with its infinite plumage variations, may puzzle the hunter and perplex the scientist, the inside of *Bonasa* is a stable, unified assembly that puts both layman and expert on solid ground.

Underneath the fuselage of skin, flesh, and feathers is a soundly structured, smoothly functioning, powerful machine. A model of good genetic engineering.

The ruffed grouse's internal anatomy, although similar to

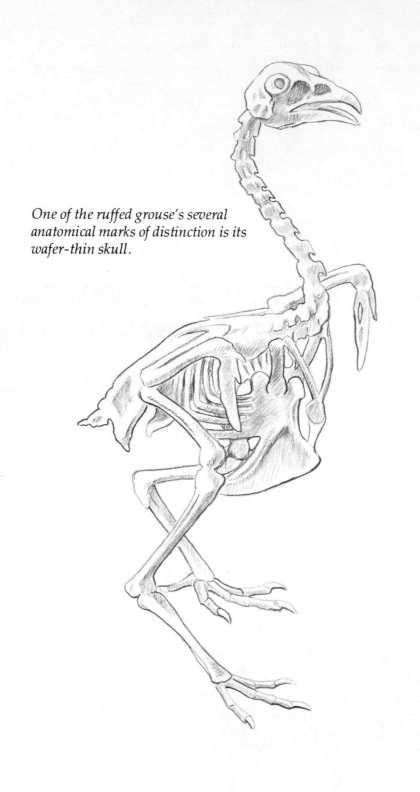

One of the ruffed grouse's several anatomical marks of distinction is its wafer-thin skull.

that of domestic fowl, has several marks of distinction. The skull of *Bonasa*, for instance, is wafer-thin compared to the chicken's or even the skulls of other species of grouse.

Dr. Arthur A. Allen, my professor in ornithology at Cornell University and a pioneer in ruffed-grouse research, illustrated some of these differences in grouse anatomy with a story about Jake, a hermit poacher, a master at his trade, who lived in the hills near Ithaca, New York.

The game warden, well aware of the poacher's out-of-season zoological transactions, was always hopeful he could get the kind of evidence that would stand up in court.

Never able to catch the poacher in the woods with illegal game in his possession, he knocked on Jake's cabin door one snowy day.

Jake opened the door. "What are you doin' around here on a day like this, Warden?" he asked, suspiciously.

"Oh, I just happened to be passing by this way—say, something smells mighty good," the warden said, glancing at two birds sizzling in a frying pan. Those birds look like grouse to me. I guess I've finally caught you with the goods, Jake."

"Now listen, Warden," Jake said, "you've got this all wrong. Them's two of my banty hens what stopped layin'. You won't find a bird shot in 'em."

"Probably because you snared them," the warden replied. "I guess you understand I'll have to take these birds for evidence. Here's your receipt."

For qualified assistance on the case, the warden took the birds to Cornell's Poultry Department. The experts had not examined grouse, but they had performed hundreds of autopsies on chickens, and examination left no doubt that the birds were not chickens. Consultation with Dr. Allen confirmed that the birds were ruffed grouse.

Since the heads had been cut off, the distinctive skulls could not be checked. But other telltale features produced prima-facie evidence that the birds were ruffed grouse: a pelvis in a higher position than in a chicken; and most distinctive of all, the sharpness of the keel-like bone structure on the underside of the vertebral column—the neck, in birds.

Another notable specialization in *Bonasa* is a muscle in the skin lying beneath each tuft of ruff feathers. Each feather follicle extends into this muscle, whose contraction causes the ruff feathers to rise away from the neck.

Shot pellets in solid-black area will result in a clean, instant kill.
Shot pellets in shaded area may disable a grouse but not necessarily kill.
Shot pellets in white area will hit nothing but feathers.
Since most of a grouse's vital organs are in its forward section, leading to the bird will bring more hits.

Every time I clean a grouse I am impressed by the small space occupied by the vital organs. So the bird is a much smaller target than it seems when viewed in the glory of full plumage.

The grouse has the conventional internal power plant of all vertebrates: kidneys, lungs, and heart—the dynamo that gives the grouse such thrust from flush through flight.

The grouse's digestive tract (its fuel line for the power plant) is organized like the answers to a pre-med student's quiz: mouth, esophagus, crop, stomach, gizzard, liver, duodenal

DIGESTIVE SYSTEM OF RUFFED GROUSE

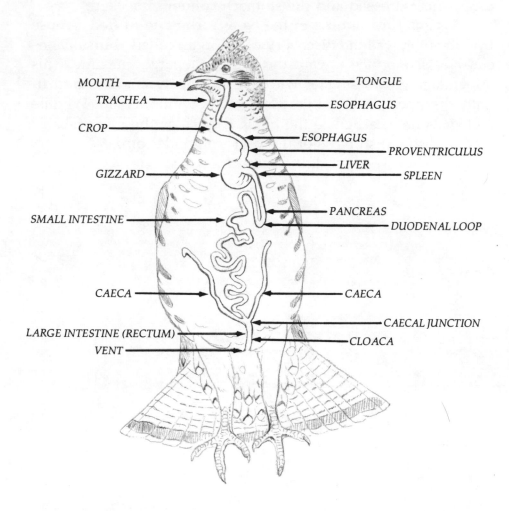

MOUTH — — TONGUE
TRACHEA — — ESOPHAGUS
CROP — — ESOPHAGUS
— PROVENTRICULUS
— LIVER
GIZZARD — — SPLEEN
— PANCREAS
SMALL INTESTINE — — DUODENAL LOOP
CAECA — — CAECA
LARGE INTESTINE (RECTUM) — — CAECAL JUNCTION
VENT — — CLOACA

loop, spleen, pancreas, small intestine, caeca, caecal junction with large intestine, cloaca, and vent.

If you bag a grouse early in a day's hunt, it pays to pull off the feathers around the crop area—an enlargement about half-way between the mouth and stomach—and cut it open. The contents will reveal the bird's food preference—at least for that day—giving you a clue to where to look for the birds.

The crop is a storage bin some of the time. But if the occasion demands, food can be bypassed directly to the stomach. So don't be surprised if you find the crop empty. If empty, the bird can be field-dressed and the stomach contents checked.

A significant finding of the New York State Ruffed Grouse Investigation was the discovery of an organ called "bursa Fabricii," a saclike pouch toward the end of the large intestine. This appendage grows smaller with age, strangely enough, and finally disappears when a grouse is about 9 months old. Wildlife biologists now recognize the bursa Fabricii as the most reliable way to distinguish birds of the year from older birds.

The bursa Fabricii grows smaller with age.

A direct outgrowth of the Investigation was the establishment of a Wildlife Research Center at Delmar, New York. Here observations on, and experiments with, pen-raised ruffed grouse produced, for the first time, information difficult or impossible to get from birds in the wild.

The Research Center found that the rate of digestion in

ruffed grouse is influenced by the kind of food the bird eats and by the air temperature.

It might seem logical to assume that a grouse reacts like a human and burns more fuel at colder temperatures, therefore increasing the digestive rate. Not so. Low air temperatures, it was discovered, slow down the bird's metabolism, which—in turn—slows digestion. Experiments showed that when the air temperature was 80° F. (27° C.), food took 107 minutes to digest; when the air temperature was 40° F. (4.5° C.), the digestive rate slowed to 242 minutes.

The reproductive system of the ruffed grouse combines the genital and urinary organs in the typical arrangement of vertebrates. The kidneys, lobed and paired, send their excretory products to the cloaca and vent through the ureter.

Since the grouse is in the resting state of the sexual cycle during the hunting season, a gunner cleaning a bird seldom spots the sex organs, which are so clearly defined during the spring breeding season.

In the male grouse, the testes, oval in shape, are located under the kidneys. Sperm passes from the testes through ducts to the cloaca and out the vent.

The female's sex organs also lie under the kidneys. Consisting of an ovary and an oviduct, they have been compared in appearance to a bunch of grapes. Normally, the ovary develops on the left side. Eggs are produced and extruded into the oviduct, where the yolk develops. The egg white is formed in the funnel-shaped tube region near the end of the oviduct, and the yellow coloring is added in the uterus.

Heart activity is an index of vitality. The stout heart of the grouse is a part of the bird's makeup that has won the heart of the hunter from the days the bird was first hunted for sport. Studies of pen-raised birds at the Research Center helped to show not only what makes a grouse tick but also how it ticks.

The average heartrate was 342 beats per minute. The rate, however, differed in males and females and varied with air temperatures, increasing when the temperature dropped. Male

birds living at 65° F. (18.5° C.) showed a heartbeat range from
295 to 306 beats per minute; females were higher, with a spread
from 358 to 367. At 40° F. (4.5° C.), the heartbeat for males
ranged from 308 to 321; females, 367 to 379.

Average heart rate of ruffed grouse is 342 beats per minute.

Under the stress of excitement—as in a bird suddenly
routed out of a piece of cover—the female of the species gets
more emotional than the male. At 40° F., the heartbeat of hens
averaged 416 beats per minute; cock birds, 391 per minute.

One series of experiments simulated the conditions of a
grouse holed up during a stormy period. Researchers withheld
food and water for periods of 100 to 148 hours. The heartbeat
rate of the grouse, instead of increasing according to the usual
physiological pattern, dropped sharply to 237.

This test of a grouse's hardiness was made under the controlled conditions of an artificial setup. It is widely known, however, that a grouse can survive the full fury of winter storms in
the wild, and that knowledge testifies to *Bonasa*'s stalwart heart.
It's a heart that every hunter, returning completely exhausted
after a hard winter day's hunt, can appreciate.

In the evolution of vertebrates, the birds are the first warm-
blooded creatures. The necessity of trying to maintain normal
body heat adds another stress to the grouse's constant struggle
for survival. So, of all the physiological factors related to a
grouse's health, body temperature is the most reliable index of

Normal body temperature of ruffed grouse is 107°F.

its well-being. The normal body temperature is about 107° F. (46° C.). However, a fluctuation pattern of body temperature takes place in a 24-hour period, the lowest temperature occurring between 11:30 P.M. and 2:30 A.M.; the highest occurring from 2:30 P.M. to 5:30 P.M.

Higher afternoon body temperature in grouse seems to be related to hunting success. From my own gunning experience, I

When a ruffed grouse gets wet, its body temperature falls quickly.

am convinced that not only are grouse more active during the post-meridian period but also that their rovings generally increase near the end of the day when light intensity fades.

Tests showed that when a ruffed grouse gets wet, its body temperature takes a big dip almost immediately and requires several hours for complete recovery. Apparently hypothermia is a hazard to the grouse as well as to the hunter.

Because of the conditions a ruffed grouse faces in the wild—summer heat waves, winter blizzards, long droughts, heavy downpours, ice, snow, and sleet—it is a tribute to the bird's life-support system and a minor miracle that a grouse survives its first year.

In back of this survival miracle is not only a strong physiological system but also a highly developed sensory apparatus.

Although a grouse has a strong tendency to sit tight, every hunter has observed that the snap of a twig or the rustle of leaves often make a grouse flush. But how do you account for the bird that goes up far ahead when the ground is wet and the walking is virtually noiseless?

The grouse probably does not have an exceptional sense of smell. In fact the olfactory lobe in the brain of all birds is small. More likely, the ruffed grouse has exceptional hearing.

Dr. John Trainer—the fellow who counted the feathers on a grouse—studied the hearing of birds as part of his work for a doctorate at Cornell University. A bird was placed in a Rube Goldberg contraption—a cage with a wired feeding tray. When the bird picked up food, it received a slight electric shock at the same time a sound of a known pitch was produced. After many repetitions, the bird became "conditioned" and reacted visibly to the sound without the accompanying electric shock. If, after many trials, the bird reacted to sounds within a certain range, but not to lower or higher tones, John assumed that the bird did not hear these tones and the hearing range of the bird was indicated.

Unfortunately, John was unable to get a ruffed grouse for testing. Among the birds he did test was a great horned owl, which responded to sounds of the lowest frequency—about 70 cycles per second—of any bird tested. We know the ruffed grouse can hear sounds of even lower frequencies, since it undoubtedly can hear its own drumming sound—40 cycles per second. Fortunately, for the grouse this sound is well below the hearing range of the owl. So the grouse is able to drum without being heard by its mortal enemy.

Since a ruffed grouse probably can hear the lowest conversational tones and the lightest footsteps, the quiet hunter is apt to be the more successful hunter.

Of all grouse senses, the sense of sight ties in most closely with the hunter's quest. Much is known about the grouse's sense of sight because the structure of the eye in all vertebrates is so similar. Long ago, it became a cliché to say the vertebrate eye is built like a camera. But that is still the most understandable way of interpreting the structure of the eye and the way it functions: a lens to converge the light rays; an iris, which is a contractable diaphragm with a variable aperture—the pupil; and a retina, which serves as the film on which an image is registered.

The eye of the ruffed grouse, like the eye in most birds, is a little flatter than the human eye. This type of eye gives a wide view, performing like a wide-angle lens in a camera.

The retina of the ruffed grouse's eye has many more light-sensitive cells (rods and cones) than has the human eye. The rods are sensitive to dim light; the cones respond to bright light and give sharp detail and color vision.

Birds of the night, like the great horned owl, have more rods than cones. Birds that are active during the day, like the ruffed grouse, have more cones than rods.

A special feature of birds, including the ruffed grouse, is the pecten, a folded tissuelike membrane that projects from the region of the optic nerve into the vitreous humor behind the lens. Some scientists believe the pecten assures the eye of sufficient nutrients and oxygen. It has also been suggested that the role of the pecten is to telegraph a warning to the brain when the slightest motion casts a shadow on the retina. If so, it's another optical

safety device making it tough for the hunter to get within shooting range.

The grouse's eye is a window of survival. For a hunter to
approach a grouse without being seen is virtually impossible.
The ruffed grouse has an unusually wide field of vision. The
bird's visual equipment enables it to see its surroundings with
both eyes or just one eye.

If you are approaching straight on, a grouse focuses both
eyes through an area in which it has the sharpest sight; if you
approach a grouse from the side, it need not even turn its head a
fraction of an inch. It will simply focus on you with the eye on
that side.

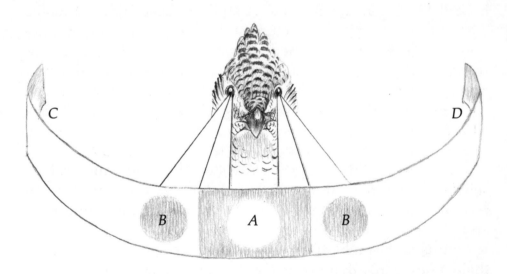

THE RUFFED GROUSE'S WIDE FIELD OF VISION

*When the ruffed grouse looks straight ahead with both eyes together, this
binocular (two-eyed) vision covers the dark oblong section of band; the central
spot (A) is the area of sharpest sight. The two shaded circles (B) indicate the
acute field of monocular vision for each eye alone. The entire band (C to D)
marks the arc of total vision of the bird.* ADAPTED FROM The Vertebrate Eye BY
GORDON L. WALLS WITH PERMISSION OF THE CRANBROOK INSTITUTE OF SCIENCE.

The eye of the grouse seems to have a built-in altimeter. When the bird plunges at jet speed from a tall pine, the eye adjusts instantly, warning the grouse when to level off and enabling it to change direction at top speed and skim along only a foot or so above the ground.

The ruffed grouse's remarkable vision was dramatically demonstrated on one of Dr. Allen's grouse hunts. As an ornithologist, the professor had a natural affection for all birds; as a hunter, he had a warm spot in his heart for gamebirds. He especially enjoyed a day in a grouse covert.

As Dr. Allen[3] tells it: "A wounded grouse I once held in my hands at the edge of a wood was obviously frightened at being caught; yet, despite its predicament, it suddenly turned its head to watch the sky. After several moments, I made out the tiniest black speck of a hawk flying so far above the earth that it was nearly out of range of human vision."

Biological feedback from research such as the work of the New York State Ruffed Grouse Investigation and studies like those carried on by the Wildlife Research Center at Delmar not only improve the wildlife biologist's knowledge of how the internal anatomy of the ruffed grouse functions but, in some instances, may be used as an aid in management.

For the hunter, a better insight into the life-force of the grouse sometimes tips the scales enough to put an extra bird in his game bag now and then. Such an awareness also deepens a hunter's appreciation of his quarry's dynamic drive.

But *Bonasa umbellus* is more than the sum of its anatomical parts. Nature has not only supplied the ruffed grouse with a marvelous inner mechanism insuring high-powered performance but has also endowed the bird with a vital spark. That spark which gives our native ruffed grouse a spirit, a character, and a personality unmatched in the gamebird world.

6

Life-Style of the Ruffed Grouse

The incredible energy generated inside this small bird translates into an intriguing life-style.

One of the most fascinating performances in nature is the courtship ritual of the ruffed grouse. This spectacular bit of woodland theater starts with the booming thunder of the cock-bird's drumming and finishes with a flamboyant strutting display of raised ruff feathers and magnificent tail spread to full fan.

To most of us, the word life-style connotes somebody's way

PARTS OF THE MATING RITUAL.
Above: Male ruffed grouse starts to drum.
Below: Male grouse in a courtship pose. Note position of the ruff.

THE ENGINE ROOM OF THE RUFFED GROUSE

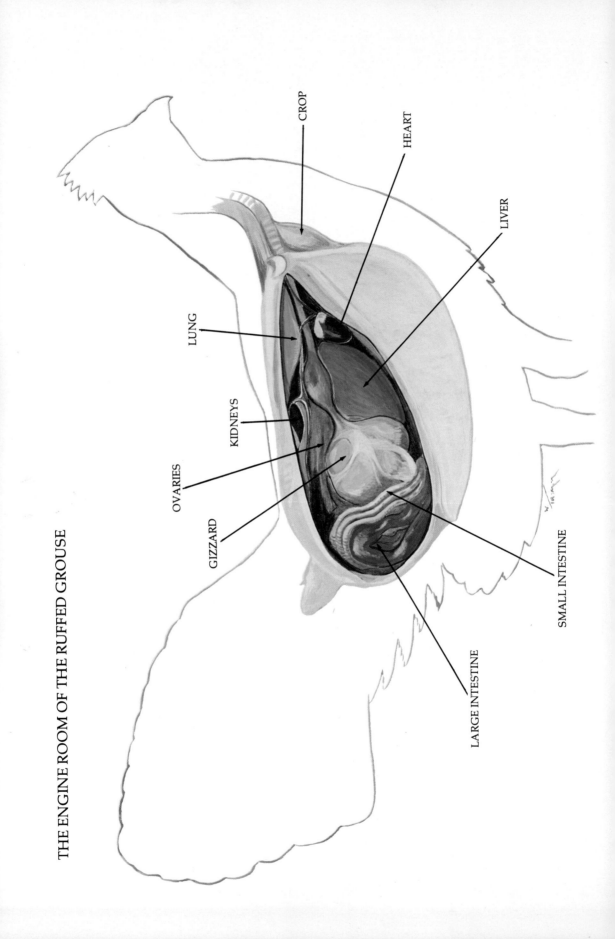

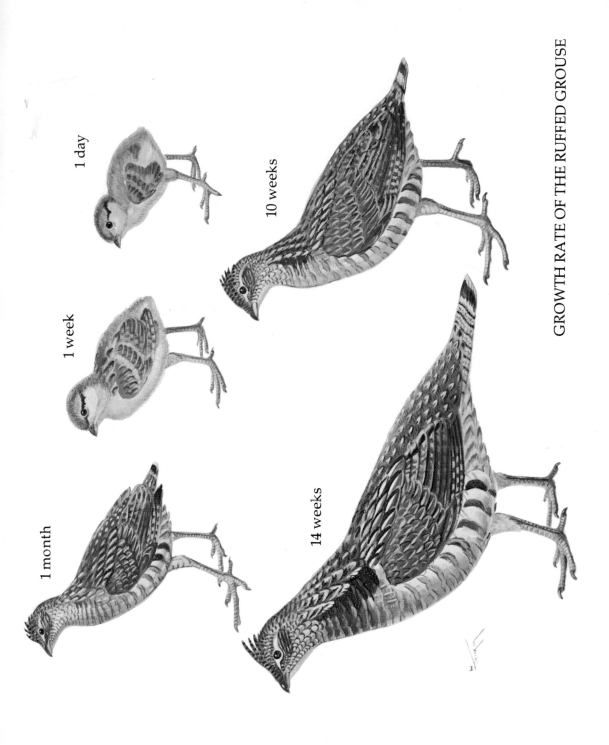

1 day

1 week

1 month

10 weeks

14 weeks

GROWTH RATE OF THE RUFFED GROUSE

A FLUSHED RUFFED GROUSE
HEADS FOR HEAVY ESCAPE COVER

FEMALE RUFFED GROUSE
WITH HER NEW BROOD

of living. The wildlife biologist interprets life-style in terms of behavior: an organism's reactions to external stimuli—like habitat, food, weather, other creatures, and its own kind; and internal stimuli—like the sexual urge, which is expressed by such behavioral patterns as its unique drumming rite.

No aspect of grouse behavior has stirred up more speculation than the "kettledrum of nature's orchestra."

Some Indian tribes believed the bird beat its wings on a log, and some tribes thought the log had to be hollow. That's a theory easily disproved: a stone wall sometimes substitutes for a log. Such a thing frequently occurs in my home coverts where stone walls, laid long ago, crisscross hilltop fields that are now grown into woodlands.

When you view the drumming of a ruffed grouse, what you think you see isn't always what's really happening. The ruffed grouse has been deceiving man with his drumming performance since their trails first crossed.

In 1752, John Bartram[7] in his letter accompanying the prototype specimen to England, noted, "they sound like thunder in the distance," and pictured the act as, "clapping their wings against their sides." A belief shared by John James Audubon[6] a century later.

Our English-oriented heritage tends to make us overlook the contributions of the early French explorers, traders, and settlers. In 1703, almost half a century before Bartram's observations, Baron de Lahontan[27] mentioned the drumming, calling it "one of the greatest curiosities of nature." He spoke of drumming as a "humming noise," and thought the sound was produced by the flapping of one wing against the other. George Edwards[20] quotes a Maryland observer: "They swell their breasts like a pouting pigeon and beat their wings."

Another viewer, possibly a relative of Baron von Münchhausen, writing in *Forest and Stream*, claimed the sound was entirely vocal—the grouse inflating a mysterious internal "air sac" and beating its wings to force air out through the mouth!

Frederick K. Vreeland,[43] after watching a grouse drum at

close range, was convinced the wings "did actually strike behind the drummer's back." Vreeland supported his contention with a series of photographs.

In 1874, William Brewster,[9] one of the first to delve seriously into the life history of the ruffed grouse, published an account of observations of a drumming grouse viewed from a blind about 12 feet from the bird. Brewster was the first to advance the theory that the drumming sound was created by the concussion of wing beats on the air. In 1923, Edmund J. Sawyer,[38] based at the Roosevelt Wildlife Station, New York State School of Forestry, came to the same conclusion.

But the controversy about the "aeolian language," as William Beebe called the drumming sound, continued in both hunting and scientific circles, the debate flaring up as one or another theory was introduced or reintroduced.

Controversy flared for years over how a male grouse makes its drumming sound.

It remained for Cornell's Dr. Allen[2] and a movie camera to settle the argument. Locating a drumming log on Connecticut Hill near Ithaca, New York, he built a blind a few feet from it and set up a movie camera at a peephole. On a chilly night in April 1929, Dr. Allen began a four-night vigil.

On the first night, a cock grouse—only the male drums— came to the drumming log at 1:40 A.M. and drummed every 5 minutes until 4 A.M. Then it moved away from the site. But the next night, the grouse—to Dr. Allen's experienced eye, the same bird—did not arrive at the log until 4 A.M. Since a male grouse may use more than one log during the courting period, perhaps he had been wooing another female at another trysting site. Again, the bird drummed at 5-minute intervals until 5:30 A.M. and departed. Although times varied, the male visited the log and drummed every night.

Despite the poor light, Dr. Allen was able to get readable

Research proved that by going through this sequence with its wingbeat, the male grouse produces a miniature sonic boom.

pictures. A drumming sequence lasted about 8 seconds, from the first wing beat to the last.

The film confirmed the conclusions of Brewster and Sawyer. Its visual evidence, in slow motion, settled once and for all the age-old argument of how the drumming sound is produced: a strong forward and upward wing beat followed by the immediate reversal of the stroke creates a vacuum into which air rushes, producing a miniature sonic boom—a small-scale version of what happens when an airplane breaks the sound barrier.

Young male grouse apparently do not drum by instinct but must learn by doing, just as a youngster practices for a place in the school band. To the observers at the Delmar Research Center, it was a comical sight to watch a frustrated young bird go through the motions without producing the sound.

Drumming is not always a romantic manifesto. *Bonasa*'s territorial imperative is strong, and drumming can also be a warning to an intruder to stay out of its domain.

Around my hilltop, I often hear the drum roll rebound off the ridges, not only in the spring, but sometimes during the summer. And occasionally I hear it during the hunting season. That sound stirs my heart and raises my hopes. I immediately start out in the direction of the booming or, rather, the direction I think the sound is coming from. I can't remember ever locating the bird. The drumming sound is deceptive in both distance and direction. The ruffed grouse is an accomplished ventriloquist. When the wind carries the sound waves toward me, the bird seems to be nearby but may be several hundred yards away or even in another quarter.

A grouse, however, seems to have no trouble in locating the sound and is always at the ready to track down the drumming of a rival bird. Some of the early market hunters worked out a stratagem "to lure jealous males" within shooting distance by imitating the drumming sound on an inflated pig bladder.

Artist Wayne Trimm, a trained wildlife biologist and an avid hunter, sits still in the woods and brings grouse close to him by taking a deep breath and beating his chest, usually with one closed fist—sometimes double-fisted, Tarzan fashion—perfectly duplicating the uncertain start, slight pause, then the throbbing rhythmic cadence increasing in a Wagnerian crescendo, finally fading out in a muffled beat. As an added realistic touch, Wayne sometimes finishes with hissing and clucking sounds.

Throughout much of the ruffed grouse's range, drumming and courtship begin in March, even before the last snows of winter are gone.

The nearest approach to the actual observation, in the wild, of the mating ritual was recorded by the ever-persevering Dr. Allen. In the course of his study of drumming, Dr. Allen placed a female grouse in a wire crate beside the drumming log. "Upon coming to the log, the male, without drumming, soon began his strutting antics, accompanied by full plumage display. This was continued for three-quarters of an hour, both on the log and on the ground beside the crate. . . . he attempted to mate with the female . . . though the wire separated them by several inches."

Wildlife biologists are shameless voyeurs and, at the Research Center, they had a good opportunity to watch the mating game and supplement Dr. Allen's observations.

Observers noted that the courtship of the male grouse is divided into three phases.

• The opening phase involves strutting, with tail fully spread and ruff raised. At this stage, the male bird calls attention to itself and dominates the scene at every opportunity. Dr. Allen called this part of the performance "intimidation display," an act accompanied by violent head-shaking and hissing. A male, often becoming extremely aggressive, would seek the most elevated spot in the pen and drum, giving the appearance of trying to maintain an exclusive territory even within the confines of the pen.

With each passing day, the males became more and more ardent; the hens became more coy, playing hard-to-get.

• Next, the cockbird underwent a noticeable personality change, marking the beginning of the second stage of courtship, the "gentle phase." Head-shaking was now less pronounced, the

*In the fighting phase of the mating
ritual, the cock grouse assumes
the "dinosaur pose."*

male moving about in a majestic manner—the epitome of a confident lover.

When the hen was ready to mate, she would do a little pos-
turing of her own, flirting openly and signaling she was in a
receptive mood by squatting in the mating position. If coition
was achieved, she hopped into her nest box to concentrate on
egg-laying.

• Now the cock entered the third and final stage—the fighting phase—of the mating ritual. Ready to take on any or all pen
mates and assuming the characteristic attitude: head and neck,
lowered and outstretched; tail, folded and dropped; feathers,
held close to the body—the "dinosaur pose."

*The base of a tree or stump was
found to be a favorite nest-
building site of female grouse.*

However, sometimes the cockbird is still in a romantic mood and seeks out another mate. He then courts and mates again. And again. One amorous Casanova mated with five females!

At the Research Center, female grouse had to accept man-made nests. On her own, in the wild, the hen molds a bowl-shaped depression on the ground and lines it with a few leaves or, occasionally, conifer needles, custom-fit to the body's contours. Simple and functional, suited to its setting like a pioneer's log cabin.

Nests measured during the course of the New York State Ruffed Grouse Investigation averaged 6¼ inches (15.9 centimeters) in diameter and 2¾ inches (7.0 centimeters) in depth. Most nests—774 out of 1158—were at the base of a tree or stump. One nest was discovered inside a stump, with access to the rotted-out interior through an old ax cut. Several nests were found under large pieces of bark, which formed a roof.

Since mating takes place in the vicinity of the drumming log, it is natural to presume that the nest will also be nearby. But of 484 nests, only 12 were within 50 feet of the log. And 225—nearly 50 percent—were more than 400 feet from the nearest drumming log.

A strong preference was noted for nesting sites in hardwood stands rather than in dense undergrowth. There was a noticeable tendency to select a gentle slope with a western exposure. And an opening near the nest, such as a logging road or a clearing, was a favored condition.

In most of the ruffed grouse's range, egg-laying takes place in April and May. During the egg-laying period, the hen wanders around a lot, sitting on the nest mostly to produce eggs. Egg-laying proceeds at the rate of 2 eggs every 3 days. A clutch varies from 9 to 14 eggs—the average, 11 eggs—taking about 17 days to complete.

If the nest is broken up after the eggs are laid, the hen will usually make another attempt to mate. Renesting clutches contain fewer eggs, averaging slightly more than 7 eggs.

Ovate—a redundant way of saying "egg-shaped"—a

ruffed-grouse egg varies in color from chalky-white to buff, often marked with olive or reddish spots. Based on a sample of 366 eggs from 30 nests, the Investigation found the average size to be $1^2/_{16}$ by $1^9/_{16}$ inches (29 by 39 millimeters).

Ruffed-grouse eggs may vary from chalky-white to buff.

After the start of incubation—which takes about 24 days—absences from the nest for feeding are infrequent, lasting from 20 to 40 minutes. Surprising though it seems, such food breaks during cold and stormy weather apparently do not affect the success of the hatch.

Despite the prolonged egg-laying period, all the chicks hatch within a day or two of one another. Under the mother, the natal down soon dries. The chicks, all fluffed up, are now presentable new members of grouse society. A Plymouth Rock chick is cute; a mallard duckling is cuter; but a ruffed-grouse chick is cutest of all.

The mother grouse, clucking proudly, steps away from the nest. With instinctive answering peeps, the chicks follow her, sometimes one at a time, sometimes several. She then leads the family on their first venture into the woodland world, never to return to the nesting site except by happenstance. Chicks unable to keep up are abandoned. From the time a ruffed grouse is born, Darwin's "survival of the fittest" rules its life.

As the chicks follow the hen, they may get cold, wet, or just plain scared and hurry to the mother hen, sliding under her for warmth and protection. But seldom the entire brood at one time. Even when only a few hours old, certain grouse demonstrate a bold spirit of independence. As Heraclitus noted, "Character is destiny." Probably these rugged individualists are the birds that will grow up to confront, confuse, and frustrate grouse hunters.

In the brood's wanderings there's much peeping and murmuring by the chicks. There's also much clucking by the hen as she sends out little communiqués of guidance and warning. Although, from a wildlife biologist's point of view, the vocal organs are primitive, grouse can produce an astonishing number of sounds, often by inflection, in an ascending or descending scale.

A mother grouse can guide, scold, or console simply by clucking. And, most important of all—she can warn. The chicks learn to scurry for cover at the first staccato cluck.

Once I startled a brood on a trail leading to the west branch of the Ausable, that marvelous trout stream in New York State's Adirondacks. The hen immediately went into her broken-wing act, at the same time sending out warning signals to the chicks. Presto, the chicks, miniature magicians, immediately performed their vanishing act.

An old hunters' tale claims that a grouse chick can grasp a leaf in its feet and roll up in it. This is pulling the long bow to the limit, but grouse have such astonishing ruses that I wouldn't dispute it. As I watched in fascination, the mother grouse suddenly took flight and buzzed around my head, missing it by inches. I moved on, but she repeated the act, diverting my attention long enough for the chicks to go into hiding before she made a slanting dive into the underbrush.

Chicks in hiding can remain silent for an amazingly long time. If some chicks get impatient before the danger is past and start peeping, the mother emits warning or scolding clucks.

Even young chicks can vary their peeps and murmurs. Most often heard is a signal that translates into: "Ma, I'm lost, where are you?"

As the chicks start their first journey, parental guidance begins almost immediately. The mother's actions and reactions demonstrate the proper behavior for a baby grouse to imitate.

Although the chicks are brooded by the mother grouse at night for a week or so, she soon teaches them, by her example, to roost. Birds only two-weeks old have been observed roosting in shrubs and on low branches in trees.

This is the time, too, the mother grouse initiates her brood into the ritual of dusting—a practical procedure for getting rid of lice and other bothersome critters. A dirt road is first choice for a dusting place, but grouse will also use bare spots in the woods and even in a tree stump's rotting wood.

The grouse was absorbed in the dusting rite and failed to notice the approaching hunter.

Once, as a fledgling hunter, I came upon a grouse in the middle of a logging road. The bird was so absorbed in the dusting rite that my entry went unnoticed. In those days, I was so gung-ho for the hunt and a bird in the game pocket that I instinctively raised my gun and fired. But pangs of conscience welled up in me as the bird thrashed around in a shower of dust.

There was nothing illegal about the act, but in grouse hunting "there is a higher law," which sets the sport apart from all other forms of gunning. Later, although the bird was roasted to a perfect golden brown, the taste of dust sullied my palate. To this day, I get a guilty feeling when I come upon a dusting grouse.

From the day ruffed grouse are hatched, a strict social hierarchy becomes established with a rigid "pecking order." Since all birds in a brood are the same age and, regardless of sex, similar in size and weight, the personality and vigor of the individual chick determines its place in the social order. Except for the top-ranking bird, each chick is dominated by a stronger member of the brood.

The low bird on the grouse totem pole—bullied physically and psychologically by the higher-ranking birds—develops an inferiority complex. Picked on, literally, as well as figuratively, the young bird bears little resemblance to the swashbuckling creature the hunter encounters in the woods. This low-ranking chick often succumbs to bodily injury or starvation.

Later, as adults, males are larger and heavier than females, so a larger proportion of males occupy the top positions in grousedom's social order.

Before young birds learn to fly, they spend all their daylight hours traveling in a closely-knit group, seldom straying more than a few feet from the hen. At no other time in its life is the ruffed grouse so gregarious as when this tightly-structured behavioral pattern prevails.

In most of its range, the brood breaks up in September, and the individualistic nature of the grouse asserts itself in a compulsion to stake out a territory of its own, ruling it with good old-fashioned woodland spunk. Wildlife biologists call this phase the "fall shuffle."

Although the carry-over birds of previous years have al-

Before they learn to fly, young ruffed grouse travel in a tight group close to the hen.

ready preempted the choice locations, occasionally an aggressive youngster will muscle in on an older grouse's territory. By contrast, an imperious old patriarch may be endowed with such an annexation compulsion that he takes over the adjoining territory of another bird.

As the shuffle works out, the higher-ranking birds in a brood will get the better territories and the best cover; the birds with inferiority hangups get the leavings. This process may ex-

During the "crazy-flight" period, ruffed grouse may fly against buildings or crash through windows.

plain why a hunter occasionally finds a grouse in unnatural cover. A ruffed grouse will occupy a territory for about three years, the bird's average life-span.*

During this fall shuffle for territories comes the "crazy-flight" period of a grouse in the wild. Even pen-raised birds at the Research Center became markedly jumpy during this same period.

A mad recklessness takes the birds far from their natural surroundings, even into the business districts of cities. On a kamikaze kick, they fly into trees and buildings and crash through windows. One bird, on its wild flight, smashed through a window in the office of the magazine *Rod and Gun in Canada.*

A grouse-hunting friend of mine had the experience of watching a frenetic bird take off, zoom into a pine thicket, and impale itself on a broken branch. A bird in the bag without even firing a shot.

Years ago, ruffed grouse frequently flew into locomotives. Now they challenge automobiles. On our country road, the yellow school bus delivers the coup de grâce. The casualties served a worthy cause: Wayne Trimm used them in working on the anatomy illustrations for this book.

Of 15 specimens of ruffed grouse that ended their lives during the crazy-flight period, the Investigation found every one was a bird-of-the-year. This fact was attested to by the presence of a bursa Fabricii—that pouch in the intestines, which is present only in young birds.

What causes the crazy flight? It must be more than just an expression of youthful spirits. A full bag of possible reasons is more overloaded with discussion than explanation.

---

*The oldest ruffed grouse on record was a banded Minnesota bird which reached an age of 7 years, 10 months. A victim of an avian predator.

The longevity record for a ruffed grouse taken by a hunter was a young-of-the-year Ohio bird, banded on August 16, 1965, and shot on January 3, 1973, attaining an age of approximately 7 years, 7 months.

"Falling leaves," claimed the *Rural New Yorker* in 1875. Certainly ruffed grouse are more edgy and harder to find on windy days; falling leaves may accentuate this restlessness. Still, this explanation is difficult to accept, considering the thousands of years and countless generations the birds have had in which to become accustomed to this natural annual occurrence.

Dr. Allen, finding infestations of stomach worms in so many crazy-flight grouse, suggested, as have others, the possibility of parasites or disease as a factor.

Some old-time hunters claim this giddy zigzagging is caused by the birds' feeding on fermented fruit—"they act like they're crocked."

That this seasonal erratic flying might be caused by inbreeding is another theory. A popular premise years ago when a "change of blood" was thought to be needed for maintaining a vigorous stock. This notion can be shot down, too. Aldo Leopold[28] noted that wild species, subject to "survival of the fittest," are of relatively pure strain, so the likelihood of any ill effects from inbreeding is much less than in domestic animals, where there is not much natural culling.

Possibly the simplest answer to crazy-flight behavior is to accept it as one of nature's mysterious ways of dispersing the broods during the fall shuffle.

The grouse, whether walking or flying, has a limited natural cruising range. Although a hunter's image of a ruffed grouse is a bird on the wing, *Bonasa* is more terrestrial than aerial. Dr. Ralph King, a pioneer in grouse research, did a study involving banded birds in Minnesota in the 1930s. He found the maximum daily cruising radius of a grouse was ½ mile and the average radius only ⅛ mile. He also found the maximum radius for an entire year was a mere 2 miles.

From what I have observed over the years, I suspect a grouse's daily travels follow a regular route on pretty much of a fixed schedule. All during one recent fall, I could depend on flushing a grouse under a lone apple tree every time I hunted the spot, just before dusk, but never at any other time.

A couple of years ago, a brood of eight birds made our yard a regular stop. Promptly at 2:00 P.M. they would appear at the side of the road, tarrying briefly for grit and salt—the remains of the highway crew's winter sanding. Then, one by one, the birds hopped over a stone wall to feed on apple drops before moving out of sight. So regular were the brood's visits that we called them our two-o'clock grouse.

Sometimes a behavioral characteristic affects a whole population unit. As grouse hunters usually discover early in their gunning, the number of birds in their favorite covert will suddenly change from a dramatic high to an abysmal low—a phenomenon known as the "grouse cycle."

Some scientists wince when they hear the term "cycle" used in connection with *Bonasa umbellus*. Its population fluctuations lack the element of a true cycle—exact predictability—such as the four-year cycle of the lemming and fox in the American Arctic.

However, records of the variations in ruffed-grouse abundance show a fairly regular syndrome of ups and downs. And such authorities as Aldo Leopold and Dr. Allen had no reservations about calling the phenomenon the "grouse cycle."

*Ruffed-grouse abundance
follows a fairly regular
path of ups and downs.*

No doubt fluctuations in animal populations were woven into nature's pattern from the very beginning of life on the planet. In recorded history, the Old Testament tells of fat years and lean years.

Early in this continent's history, lean years resulted in edicts prohibiting the taking of ruffed grouse at any time: in 1708, New York; in 1721, the Province of Quebec; and in 1814, the Province of New Brunswick.

In his letter to George Edwards[20] around 1750, John Bartram wrote about the scarcity of birds in the Philadelphia area. That scarcity might have been due, he speculated, to "the encroachments of civilization in the lower settlements of Pennsylvania."

Around 1830, Thomas Nuttall,[33] Boston ornithologist traveling in New England, reported: "Not a single bird of the species was now to be seen. . . . they have no doubt migrated southward."

Generally speaking, the periods of abundance get less attention than periods of scarcity. But one nineteenth-century market-hunting item caught my eye because the locale it mentioned was near my home coverts. In 1875, some 2500 birds were shipped by railroad to New York out of Poughkeepsie. That must have been a bonanza year for ruffed grouse in our area.

Dr. Ralph King, through painstaking research, was able to trace the history of the grouse cycle in Minnesota back to 1870. But more complete records have been kept on *Bonasa*'s population fluctuations since 1900. Further studies of the grouse cycle in the United States have been made in Minnesota; also in Connecticut, Maine, Massachusetts, Michigan, New Hampshire, New York, Pennsylvania, Vermont, and Wisconsin; and in Canada, in the provinces of New Brunswick, Nova Scotia, and Ontario.

The collected data clearly confirm what has long been obvious to grouse hunters: a high level of abundance is followed by a period of extreme scarcity—a pattern occurring with some degree of regularity. These statistics show that periods of scarcity occur at intervals of nine to ten years; peak periods occur at intervals of eight to twelve years. During the lows, the sport of grouse hunting turns sour, like wine to vinegar.

The kicker in the grouse cycle is that periods of scarcity have not happened uniformly and simultaneously throughout the bird's range, and the same sort of inconsistency is true of the peak periods. The nearest approach to uniformity were the continent-wide scarcities in 1907 and 1914. But even in those years, numerous regional pockets, contrary to the general trend, contained a good crop of birds. And in adjoining areas, such as Minnesota and Wisconsin, the highs and lows do not always coincide.

I am inclined to think that such variations may also apply to smaller geographical units. My home coverts straddle two watersheds: to the east, the Harlem Valley; to the west, the Hudson Valley. Several times in the last three decades, grouse have been scarce on the Harlem Valley side but noticeably more plentiful on the flanks of the Hudson Valley, just a few miles away.

Although past trends of grouse populations can be plotted, future ups and downs are difficult to forecast. But the downswing of the grouse cycle is always associated with the failure of an annual increment to replace the brood stock. The birds-of-the-year simply do not survive to their first breeding season and, frequently, not even to the hunting season.

What causes the failure is a perennial cracker-barrel topic for gunners and a puzzle to wildlife biologists. Imaginative suppositions range from Nuttall's "mass migration" theory, to sunspots, to the far-out possibility that it is one of the effects of the electromagnetic energy surrounding us.

The sunspot theory as it affects the cyclic nature of grouse populations may not be such a wild conjecture after all if we think about the effects on the weather. Robert W. Darrow,[15] one of the four authors of *The Ruffed Grouse* published by the New York State Conservation Department, in discussing weather, states: "Regardless, however, of what governs it (weather), or to what extent it may or may not be related to the forces represented by sunspot changes, the evidence is becoming increasingly strong that weather is a primary factor in governing variations in grouse abundance."

U.S. Weather Bureau temperature records from 1890 to 1942, plotted against known periods of scarcity in New York

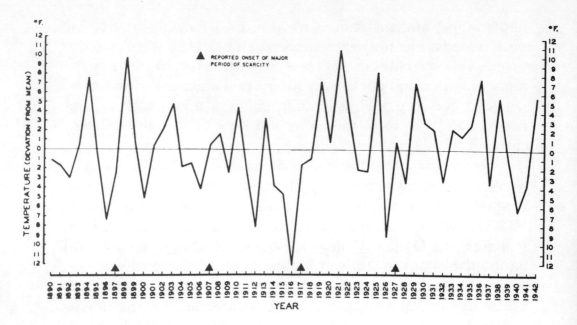

WEATHER AND FLUCTUATIONS OF GROUSE POPULATIONS

Relationship (sum of deviations from the mean) of March and June air temper-atures to beginnings of ruffed-grouse scarcity in New York State. COURTESY NEW YORK STATE DEPARTMENT OF ENVIRONMENTAL CONSERVATION.

State, show that when New York temperatures were unusually low in either March or June or both, a period of scarcity invari-ably followed. It is significant that no major decline has been recorded in New York that was not preceded by colder-than-average weather in either or both of these months.

However, trying to correlate weather with the grouse cycle is difficult, as Walter F. Crissey[12]—another of the authors of *The Ruffed Grouse*—discovered in the course of making this study: "In the first place, it comprises a number of components: tem-perature, precipitation, sunshine, and humidity, to mention a few. But more important are the high variability of these forces, the rapidity with which they fluctuate and the fact that their pat-tern is constantly changing."

But the true scientist comes out in Crissey's own appraisal of his analysis; also recognition of the part *Bonasa*'s adaptability plays in the evaluation of weather influences: "One must bear in mind that this (weather) is only one factor affecting grouse abundance and other influences may outweigh it.

"The standard measurements of the Weather Bureau are taken by means of instruments placed on a platform six feet above the ground in an open spot. . . . thus the shaded thermometer at a 'weather station' may register 20 degrees below zero, but if a grouse occupies a protected nook on a sunny slope during the day and resorts to a snow-roost at night, it has succeeded, to a considerable extent, in minimizing the effect of that temperature."

In the hot-stove league, hunters are apt to blame predators more than weather when grouse are scarce. Hawks, owls, and foxes are popular targets. The remains of grouse found in the woods would seem to be conclusive evidence. But to wildlife biologists, whose studies of stomach analyses have proved that grouse are not a staple item in the diet of any of *Bonasa*'s predators, this premise is not valid.

The dead grouse that hunters find in the woods are sometimes victims of disease or parasites—another factor considered a possible cause of cyclic scarcity.

During the New York State Ruffed Grouse Investigation, autopsies were performed on 1728 adult grouse and 1119 chicks from all parts of the state.

Based on these examinations and other observations on pathological conditions, the Investigation concluded that disease should certainly be recognized as one of the factors limiting grouse abundance. But no strong evidence was uncovered pointing to a causative relationship between disease and cyclic fluctuations in the level of grouse abundance.

Although the grouse cycle continues to be largely a riddle, new tools and new techniques are helping to uncover fresh facts about the grouse's life-style. One helpful invention is the mirror trap, an improved device for capturing grouse alive, especially drumming males. Another aid is the use of taped recordings of drumming, planted at strategic locations to lure grouse of both sexes.

Then there's radio tracking, which has hatched the new science of "biotelemetering." The miracles of electronics have come to *Bonasa's* world.

A grouse can now be "bugged." Radio tracking is a modern technique that makes it possible to determine the location of a particular grouse at any one time and keep a continuous log of the bird's travels.

At Cloquet Forest Research Center—Cloquet has replaced New York State's Connecticut Hill as the outstanding outdoor ruffed-grouse laboratory—William H. Marshall[31] and his associates have designed a radio-frequency (RF) marking and tracking system to gather information previously limited to sporadic observations.

The tracking system has two basic elements: 1) an RF marker, which is a transmitter, battery, and harness for the bird, and 2) a portable receiver.

Using 12 markers and 4 receivers, a crew of 4 men maintained contact with a dozen birds during a 60-day period—the field-tested life of the transmitter's battery.

It should be pointed out that some wildlife biologists believe that radio-tracking studies as they apply to ruffed grouse have a limited value because of the difficulty of working with large numbers of birds. But because the birds are undisturbed by the presence of field workers, biotelemetering probably provides a truer record of their habits than general observation.

In many cases, the new technique confirms facts originally determined by the classic approach of simple observation. Kudos to the talents of the pioneering workers of the 1920s and 1930s—long before the electronic era.

Marshall reports an interesting finding uncovered by the new technique: "As shown by the telemetry studies, the feeding of ruffed grouse during the winter and spring occurs over very short periods in the morning and evening and is highly selective toward the flower buds of staminate aspen trees. . . . by feeding rapidly on the buds . . . for short periods of time, the birds choose a very rich source of food while minimizing energy loss."

One unexpected dividend of the research: the discovery that the transmitter's signals varied with a bird's activities. The pitch of the "beeps" distinguished walking, running, flying, feeding, drumming, and resting.

The more optimistic wildlife biologists hope that eventually they will be able to monitor a grouse's muscular responses, heartbeat, and respiratory rate, which will provide information about grouse in the wild as has already been established for pen-raised birds at New York State's Research Center.

As a professional conservationist, I have a natural interest in these new techniques and what they disclose about *Bonasa*'s behavior.

As a hunter, I'm always eager to learn more about the life-style of the grouse to improve my chances of locating birds.

But as one captivated by nature, I hope some of the mystery surrounding the grouse will always remain—mystery that adds so much to the appeal of this remarkable bird.

7
Cover:
Food/Shelter

The ruffed grouse is a bird of the woodlands and the brushy thickets. Grouse hunting is no groomed-terrain recreation but a rough and tough backcountry sport.

During the open season, a grouse hunter can always spot another grouse hunter, even in mufti at the neighborhood tavern. Most often it's the telltale scratches on the back of the hands. Sometimes it's the scarlet line decorating his cheek. An honor badge—as esteemed as a Heidelberg scar—showing he has been deep in grouse coverts. Those coverts are furnished with wall-to-wall briers, but a hunter must penetrate them if he wants to maintain a satisfactory success ratio.

The grouse is locked into a complex ecological niche. Grouse cover divides into several natural cover types: 1) open land; 2) overgrown brushy land; 3) hardwoods, second-growth and mature; 4) conifers; and 5) cutover areas or slashings. A productive covert is made up of a favorable combination of cover types to meet the basic needs of the ruffed grouse: shelter, food, and breeding sites.

In American gunning circles, the terms "cover" and "covert" have long been used interchangeably, both meaning a specific area on which game is hunted.

To the wildlife manager, and increasingly so to the hunter, cover refers to the vegetative makeup of a larger geographic unit, the covert. You might refer, for instance, to "a good piece of cover in the Lower Forty covert."

Cover may consist of a dozen or more botanicals. Or a single species like a lone pine tree used as an overnight roosting spot— especially if it adjoins a feeding ground.

But grouse cover is not a stable commodity. It has a life of its own—a dynamic, ever-changing existence. Foresters call this natural phenomenon "forest succession" because vegetative growth is always advancing to the next stage.

Since *Bonasa* is found over such a vast range, the species of plant life vary considerably in different sections, but the process and pattern are the same.

The forest-succession clock can be set back to zero by clearcutting. But the cleared land does not remain bare for long. There's a constant barrage of seeds, and young shoots engage in a struggle for dominance. First to take hold are the weeds and grasses that can survive direct exposure to the sun. Next come the woody shrubs and berry bushes, major producers of food. Finally emerging are the tree species, eventually growing up to form a closed canopy—the climax stage, which snuffs out the undergrowth, the bread box of the ruffed grouse. And, unfortunately, the climax stage is a stable one, which continues unless clear-cutting starts up the forest succession process again.

During the past 30 years, I have observed forest succession at first hand. On our hilltop, for over a century, farmers carried on a simple type of agriculture. Every farm had some pasture land and fields in a corn-oats-hay rotation. These farms, which were virtually self-sustaining units, each had a dooryard vegetable garden, an orchard, and a woodlot where the annual cutting of sections for firewood assured future blocks of brushy areas for grouse. Such cutting also created edge-cover, the core of good grouse hunting.

But in time, with depletion of our hilltop's thin soil, farming became more and more marginal. A gradual abandonment began—an exodus accelerated by World War II. Young men left the farms for the service, and the older men went to factories for a more assured way of earning a living. They did not return to their farms again. Though these farms were hardscrabble for farmers, they were at the peak stage of plant succession for ruffed grouse.

For anybody to be set down in this grouse gunners' paradise was a miraculous spin of fortune's wheel. Good coverts were pieced together like a huge patchwork quilt. I could fan out in any direction and hunt acres and acres of brush land that was loaded with foods to suit a grouse's taste. Adjoining were sections of hardwoods in various stages of succession, many just right for nesting; some sections were interspersed with small natural stands or reforested blocks of conifers, which offered fine winter cover. Nearby pastures closed into grassy bays and berry patches; and abandoned orchards drew birds as a honey tree draws bears.

But gradually the inexorable process of succession is creeping into my favorite coverts. In the "hot corner," the final stage of succession is closing in. The maples, birches, and pines have grown large enough to shade the undergrowth. So the thick clumps of junipers and tangles of blackberry bushes are disappearing. So, too, are my wine-and-roses days of grouse hunting.

But the energy shortage may brighten up this gloomy grouse-hunting scene. Now it is not only practical to burn wood but also a kind of status symbol. The old-time wood-burning stoves are having a revival as auxiliary heating units in thousands of homes in parts of the ruffed grouse's range.

Again, the woodlot is playing an important role in our day-to-day living. What is a boon to *Homo sapiens* may be the salvation of *Bonasa umbellus*. Cutting and clearing are improving the food-shelter support system on thousands of acres of grouse cover.

As *Bonasa*'s persona is more complex than that of most other gamebirds, so are its cover requirements. A ringneck pheasant, for instance, can live, breed, and die in a hundred-acre hayfield. But for the grouse, a covert composed of just one type of cover, even the most favorable, is virtually worthless.

And the grouse's cover requirements vary with the age of the bird, the weather, and the seasons.

In the spring at nesting time, a grouse's fancy turns to woodlands, preferably second-growth hardwoods.

During the summer, when the broods are still intact, the

The buds of deciduous trees are staple winter food for ruffed grouse.

cover sought is diverse. Especially favored by the whole grouse family are young hardwoods. The birds take excursions for daily rations to cutover areas and to overgrown, brushy lands—especially berry bushes and weed patches.

When winter arrives, grouse seek the thick shelter of the evergreens in much of its range. Conifers, which have been used during the summer and fall as roosting sites, now become vitally important, full-time cover. The choicest locations adjoin stands of deciduous trees whose buds are staple winter food. In the Midwest, aspen is the most important—both as cover and as food. And sometimes, of course, instead of roosting in trees, grouse find that a blanket of snow serves as a snug shelter.

In my coverts, where the birds have a choice of cover— hemlock, pine, or cedar—hemlock, possibly because it is more abundant, seems to be first choice and pine a close second. One winter bastion adjoins an old apple orchard, and sometimes on my winter walks I will spot a bird "budding" in a tree.

Knowing a grouse's whereabouts in spring, summer, and winter is a professional concern to the wildlife biologist. But the grouse hunter is more interested in where the birds are in autumn.

Hedgerows, brushy patches, wild grape tangles, and, of course, apple orchards are good bets in early fall. Later, birds favor woodlands, especially if there are oak and beech trees and it's a mast year with acorns and beechnuts plentiful.

There's one more type of shelter. Escape cover. This fact is something not learned from textbooks but acquired with experience by every grouse hunter who hunts a covert often enough to become acquainted with an individual bird. The smartest grouse seem to select a territory with a good escape hatch in mind. When *Bonasa* is flushed, its strong survival instinct and innate cunning impel it toward a vegetative fortress such as a bit of blowdown, a juniper cluster, or a laurel patch.

For a couple of seasons, I had a regular rendezvous with a grouse that flushed from a side-hill bunch of thorn apples, always just out of range. Then the bird headed for the eye of an adjoining covert and invariably sailed into a cat's cradle piece of cover: burdock, barberry, and blackberry bushes guarding a swamp whose footing was as treacherous as quicksand. I was never able to reflush the bird from this sanctum. That grouse seemed to disappear into the nowhere—a botanical Bermuda Triangle.

Good grouse cover has not only the plant life for a protective habitat but also the vegetation to provide essential food.

Sometimes food cover is temporary shelter. In my area, viburnums are plentiful. In early fall, grouse gorge on the berries, not even leaving at dusk but staying at the source of supply and roosting in the bushes at night. During the day when I'm on a hunt and approaching a clump, the telltale swaying of slim branches informs me that a grouse, even though out of view, is feeding.

An adult grouse is primarily a vegetarian. A gallinaceous bird, it's classified in the same scientific group, Galliformes, as most of the other gamebirds and domestic fowls of the world. Because these birds spend most of their feeding time on the ground, they are known as "scratchers."

In its search for food, *Bonasa* may be a seed feeder, a leaf gatherer, a gleaner, a berrypicker, a wild-grape harvester and apple eater, and—in winter—a browser subsisting chiefly on buds, catkins, and twigs.

One of the first in-depth studies of the food of ruffed grouse was made in 1923 by Thomas Smyth,[41,42] a graduate student of Dr. Arthur Allen at Cornell. In a rare instance of education and sport teaming up in a worthy cause, Dr. Allen, a keen grouse hunter, spent many hours in the coverts getting specimens for Smyth. Smyth also had Dean Price and Professor Hutchinson of Virginia Military Institute and Dr. John Greeley of the New York State Conservation Department—real high-powered help—collecting birds.

Dr. Smyth's work guided the New York State Ruffed Grouse Investigation when the group undertook a study of grouse food.

The Investigation, in analyzing the stomach contents of 1000 birds, discovered *Bonasa* was a real trencherman. One grouse crop was filled with 1197 tree buds, 267 fruit seeds, 160 catkins, and the remains of speedwell, hawkweed, and strawberry leaves.

The grouse eats not only a tremendous quantity but also an amazing variety. An examination of 1000 crops revealed 994 different kinds of food, representing 334 species.

Food can also provide all the water requirements of the ruffed grouse. The New York State Ruffed Grouse Investigation concluded that the birds normally can find satisfactory amounts of water from one source or another in succulent foods with a high moisture content (such as fruits and aspen leaves), augmented by dew.

Despite thousands of sightings, the Investigation never observed a wild adult grouse drinking from open water. And in all my years of hunting, I have never seen a grouse drinking water; nor have I ever met a hunter who has.

Surprisingly, many poisonous plants apparently have no toxic effect on ruffed grouse. Mountain laurel, harmful to many animals, including man, is eaten in quantity by grouse, especially in winter. Even the deadly nightshade is not shunned; and Dr. Smyth reported 280 poison-ivy berries in one bird.

From the point of view of a good knife-and-fork man, I can tell you that what a grouse eats will affect the flavor of the meat when it comes to the table.

Daniel Elliott,[21] an English writer traveling in this country in the late nineteenth century, wrote about the ruffed grouse of the Pacific Northwest: "The flesh is white and palatable save in winter when it is often bitter, occasionally flavored with turpentine from eating the buds of the fir trees."

In contrast, John James Audubon's great rival, Alexander Wilson,[47] declared: "The bird is in the best order for the table in September and October. In this season they feed chiefly on whortleberries and the little red aromatic partridge-berries, the last of which gives their flesh a peculiar delicate flavor."

My taste buds are offended when I eat a bird that has been

feeding on juniper berries. But a bird that has been dining on beechnuts is food to caress the palate, worthy of a Chambertin of the best vintage.

Differences in diet naturally vary in different parts of the bird's range and from year to year, depending on the relative abundance provided by nature. But the great bulk of the grouse's diet comes from aspens, birches, cherries, and hophornbeam.

Grouse diets also vary with the season. In the spring, a New York State grouse's menu—according to the Investigation's findings—consists chiefly of aspen, cherry, and apple buds; catkins of birch and hophornbeam—known as ironwood to most hunters—and the buds and leaves of mountain laurel.

When the snow melts, ruffed grouse will pick up beechnuts left over from the previous autumn.

As the snow melts, beechnuts, left over from autumn, are picked up; so are acorns, which swell the bird's crop grotesquely like a goiter. Strawberry leaves soon furnish the first greens of the season.

Springtime is hatching time, a period in which age makes a distinct difference in a grouse's eating habits. During the first two weeks, the young chicks, instead of being vegetarians like their elders, feed almost exclusively on insects. This diet phenomenon is possibly caused by the need for a high-protein diet at this stage. A grouselet's menu has nearly 600 insect species. Leading the list are ants, wasps, sawflies, beetles, grasshoppers, and crickets.

During the summer, the entire grouse family feasts on the bountiful treats of the season. Most commonly eaten are the fruits of the blackberry, raspberry, cherry, strawberry, and partridgeberry; the leaves of aspen; and the seeds of the sedges, maples, and jewelweed.

Although winter seldom brings an actual shortage of grouse food, it does bring a dull diet, a diet limited almost entirely to buds and catkins. This fare is seasoned now and then with lingering fruits like the sumac.

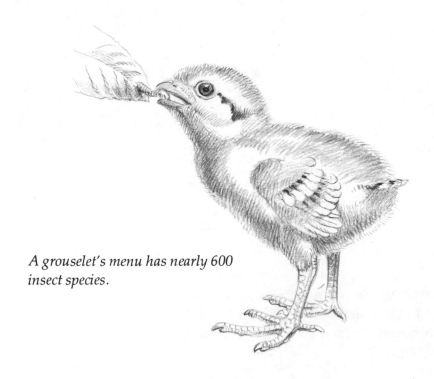

A grouselet's menu has nearly 600 insect species.

A grouse's winter menu may be monotonous but *Bonasa* doesn't suffer from malnutrition. Most buds and catkins contain vital protein: hazelnut buds, about 26 percent; aspen and hophornbeam buds, 9 percent; and apple buds, 8 percent.

The buds and catkins of birch, hazelnut, and hophornbeam are common winter foods. Also the buds of aspen, cherry, shadbush, and apple.

In fact, it was *Bonasa*'s wintertime habit of "budding" in apple trees that once caused this noble bird to be listed as a varmint. Around 1880, some Massachusetts towns put a bounty of 25 cents on ruffed grouse in an effort to protect farmers' orchards. And, as late as 1924, the State of New Hampshire paid $26,800 in damage claims.

Good grouse cover supports good grouse hunting.

An ability to read cover is one of the greatest assets a grouse hunter can acquire. I learned from Old Ed, a turn-of-the-century market hunter who became my grouse-hunting mentor during my salad days with the State Conservation Department. Old Ed taught me not to ramble-scramble around grouse coverts aimlessly.

"Stop every now and then," he said, "and size things up."

The art of sizing up a cover was a trade skill of market hunters, and Old Ed had an uncanny knack for sensing a "birdy" spot.

On one of our early hunts, Ed and I were walking along the edge of a bramble when a grouse went up ahead and flew into an adjoining woods. When we came to the place we had last seen the bird, Old Ed pulled up short and glanced around. To me, it all looked the same—a typical scene of leafless woodland in late November.

Old Ed pointed to a tiny patch of weeds my eye had missed completely. "I'll bet our bird is in there," he declared with a confidence I could not share. But it was.

"How could you be so sure?" I asked, as he added the bird to his belt carrier.

"That's somethin' I don't think you can say," he replied. "It's somethin' you get after you've chased pa'tridge as many years as I have."

Fall is the season the hunter enters the grouse's world, seeing firsthand the interrelationships of cover—the close tie between shelter and food—at a time they are most readily recognized.

FAVORITE FALL FOODS OF RUFFED GROUSE IN NORTH-EASTERN NORTH AMERICA

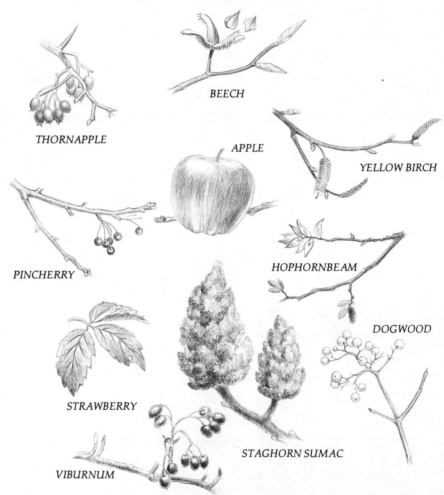

BEECH

THORNAPPLE

APPLE

YELLOW BIRCH

PINCHERRY

HOPHORNBEAM

DOGWOOD

STRAWBERRY

STAGHORN SUMAC

VIBURNUM

BASED ON ILLUSTRATION FROM The Ruffed Grouse *BY GARDINER BUMP, ROBERT W. DARROW, FRANK C. EDMINSTER, WALTER F. CRISSEY. COURTESY NEW YORK STATE DEPARTMENT OF ENVIRONMENTAL CONSERVATION.*

A hunter who knows the favorite fall foods of grouse will know where to look for birds.

Autumn is harvest time not only for man but also for the grouse. *Bonasa* spends most of the day feeding, putting on extra weight as a kind of security blanket against the long winter ahead.

Grouse now feast on the fruits of fall: the apple, thornapple, and sumac, the viburnum and the dogwoods. Three species of cherry—pin, black, and choke—furnish a sizable part of the grouse's fall diet.

Beechnuts, in bearing years, will pull in birds during the fall about the way a lodestone attracts a compass needle. But trying to steal up on a grouse feeding under a beech tree is far from a sure thing. In the sparse cover of the leafless autumn wood-lands, a grouse will flush long before a hunter can get within shooting range.

A few years ago, the au-thor noticed that ruffed grouse were on a binge of eating barberries.

A grouse sometimes gets a yen for a food seldom a part of its diet. A few years ago, I noticed the grouse were on a barberry kick. During a day's hunt, I noticed that more than half of the birds were flushed from barberry bushes, which are often stripped clean early in the fall. At the time, I thought this prefer-ence was simply because the berries were so plentiful. But for a couple of years after that, although the bushes hung heavy with the bright red berries, they remained untouched even in winter. Just another example of the grouse's persnickety ways.

Important findings have been made in recent years about grouse preferences for food and shelter. Early investigators, of course, recognized the value of aspen buds and catkins as a common grouse food. But Gordon W. Gullion, who is considered one of the leading authorities on ruffed grouse in North America today, has uncovered a larger, more significant role of aspen in the life of a grouse. His findings are based on 22 years' research, mostly at the Minnesota School of Forestry's Research Center near Cloquet.

"This work," notes Gullion,[25] "has shown that at one point or another during the life of an aspen stand, these trees meet all the annual cover and food requirements of ruffed grouse. No other forest tree does this.

"In its primary stage, dense young aspen sucker regeneration provides the best possible cover for a hen and her chicks. Then as natural thinning reduces the density of the stand, and the trees reach a height of 25 to 30 feet, this same aspen stand loses its value as brood cover but becomes a high-quality cover for wintering and breeding grouse. An aspen stand usually is 8 to 12 years old when this occurs. At this stage, the cover is open enough for adult grouse to operate easily but still too dense to give predators easy access to the birds. Natural thinning continues as less vigorous trees lose their race towards the sun, and usually at about 25 to 30 years of age, the aspen stand becomes so open that winged predators have easy access to the grouse and it loses its value as cover. But this aged aspen is still important, for at 30 to 35 years, the male flower buds produced annually by aspen, become a favored and probably critical winterlong food resource for ruffed grouse. This value remains until the stand is cut and its cycle begins again."

Aspen's value for ruffed grouse is especially significant because of the species' wide distribution—the most widely-distributed forest tree in North America. Moreover, the aspen's range

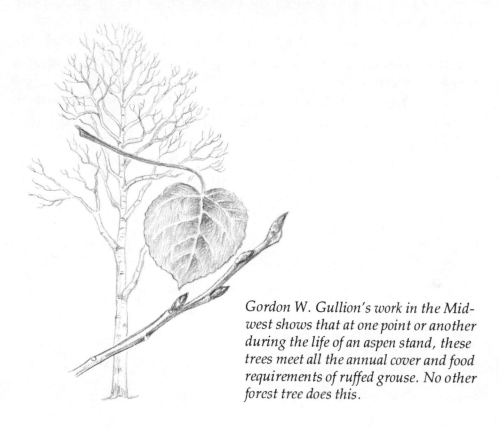

Gordon W. Gullion's work in the Mid-west shows that at one point or another during the life of an aspen stand, these trees meet all the annual cover and food requirements of ruffed grouse. No other forest tree does this.

almost duplicates that of *Bonasa:* from the tree line of Alaska to Labrador, across all of Canada, and from California to New England and south through the Appalachians.

The practical research of Gordon Gullion and his associates not only adds to our knowledge of the ruffed grouse's cover and food requirements but also enriches our understanding of this great American gamebird's way of life.

To watch *Bonasa* feeding in its natural setting is a priceless privilege for a grouse hunter. Once while resting near the top of a knoll, I looked down through a narrow draw as a magnificent brown bird sauntered into view, plumage radiant in the noonday sun. Accepting me as part of the landscape, the bird, circling a thornapple, searched for food. An intensity of purpose marked every movement; its bearing had dignity and a stately grace.

No true grouse hunter could ever break up such a scene with a leaden shower.

The interwoven ecological threads of the plant life that fills the bird's biological needs make up the fascinating fabric of a grouse covert.

But it is when *Bonasa umbellus* comes on stage that this woodland tapestry comes to life. Then the whole scene lights up, filling a covert with beauty and excitement.

As Aldo Leopold[29] phrased it: "In terms of conventional physics, the grouse represents only a millionth of either the mass or the energy of an acre. Yet subtract the grouse and the whole thing is dead."

8
Ruffed-Grouse
Management

The management of the ruffed grouse is both a science and an art. As a science: analyzing and coordinating facts learned about *Bonasa*'s natural history, physiology, behavior, and environmental needs. As an art: applying this knowledge to produce a satisfactory feathered crop for recreational use.

Although management procedures are similar for all species of game, it seems to me that the complex nature of the ruffed grouse and the complexity of its requirements make managing the bird a great challenge.

Ruffed-grouse management is at its best when it teams up with research. This cross-fertilization can produce helpful bio-feedback. More and more, a harvest of grouse depends on a harvest of facts.

Laws to regulate the hunter were among early attempts to protect grouse populations.

From the beginning, the tools of grouse management have followed the conventional sequence: laws to protect grouse populations by regulating the hunter; measures to control predators; establishment of game refuges; replenishment through artificial propagation and the use of environmental controls.

Protecting game by management of the hunter through laws had its beginnings in tribal taboos. These taboos became accepted as unwritten laws. And unwritten laws were given legal clout eventually, when writing became a form of communication.

Probably the earliest written law to conserve wildlife was included in the Mosaic Law of the Old Testament: "If a bird's nest chance to be before thee. . . . with young ones, or eggs, and the dam sitting upon the young, or upon the eggs, thou shalt not take the dam with the young. . . ."

Centuries later, in England, when the land barons exacted the Magna Charta from King John at Runnymede in 1215, the ownership of *"ferae naturae"* underwent a fundamental change. The king no longer owned wild game as a divine right but now held it in sacred trust as a representative of the people.

But as far as making the blood sports of England more democratic was concerned, the Great Charter was more a victory for semantics. Hunting remained pretty much the prerogative of royalty and the landed gentry. "The noble of every age," observed Honoré de Balzac, "has done his best to invent a life which he and only he can live."

Strangely enough, the Magna Charta probably held more benefits for the hunters of America than for their counterparts in England. When the English colonists came to the land of the ruffed grouse, paramount in their minds was a determination to establish and preserve individual freedoms—including the freedom to hunt. The colonists had an entirely new concept of the chase—public hunting—an idea as revolutionary as the Declaration of Independence.

Throughout the 1600s, all of North America was a freewheeling hunting society. Ruffed grouse were so plentiful, and hunters so few, no legal controls were needed. A hunter was free to hunt the bird 365 days a year with a bonus day in leap year.

But this hunter's paradise could not last. America's growing population gradually took over much game habitat, and the heavy harvesting of grouse for food caused local scarcities.

Furthermore, periodic population declines of ruffed grouse began to be noticed. Unaware of the "grouse cycle," the Americans believed shortages were caused by overshooting. They also thought a law prohibiting the hunting of ruffed grouse for a period of time would restore huntable populations.

The first closed season on ruffed grouse was declared by the Province of New York in 1708. In 1721, Quebec declared a closed season— "an ordinance to prevent the destruction of partridge." In 1818, Massachusetts enacted a closed season on ruffed grouse. New York had its second closed season in 1839; Ohio took similar action in 1857.

But it was not until shortly after 1900 that New York, and most of the other northeastern states, abolished market hunting, the use of traps and snares, and spring shooting. Around this time New York also established a seasonal bag limit—a generous one of 36 on ruffed grouse.

Legal hunting seasons did not open until fall. The closed season protected the birds during the breeding and brooding months, thus establishing the present tradition of fall grouse hunting, purely as a sport.

The ruffed grouse, however, has such an extensive range that hunting seasons vary with geography. A recent check shows that in a section of Alaska, August marks the earliest opening of the grouse season; Oregon, too, has an August opening in some areas. Michigan and Minnesota have September openings.

In most parts of the ruffed grouse's range, however, October marks the beginning of the gunning season. Of the 34 states that offer ruffed-grouse hunting, the majority have October openings. In Canada, season openings are divided between September and October.

Virginia does not open its grouse season until November, as does Kentucky and South Carolina; and New Jersey opens in December—the latest of all.

Seasons vary in length from less than a month, as in Oregon, to 8 months in the Northwest Territories, and 9½ months in a section of Alaska.

As for the effect of hunting-season length on the annual grouse harvest, game managers may have to revise their thinking.

Walter L. Palmer and Carl L. Bennett, Jr.[35] carried on a study through a grouse cycle on Michigan's Rifle River Area—the site, once every three years, of the Grand National Grouse Dog Championship trial. The authors conclude: "Kill data for the Area, which receives up to four times as much hunting pressure as other comparable areas in Michigan, suggest that a much longer hunting season would not substantially increase the grouse kill. Thus, a greatly extended hunting season on a state-wide basis would seem to be readily justifiable."

Daily bag limits, at this writing, range from as few as two birds in some states to no limit at all in the Northwest Territories.

The Province of Alberta, in an unusual approach, determines its daily bag limit on ruffed grouse on an ecological and sociological basis: "Our management technique is one based on setting an arbitrary limit of 10 and depends on the law of diminishing returns to limit hunting as the population declines. The decline, as far as we can tell at present, is not related to hunting pressure but to a complex relationship to predators and the hare-lynx, horned owl, etc. cycle."

A seasonal limit is only as effective as the hunter's personal code of conduct. Most states have abandoned this regulation. Exceptions at present are Virginia with a seasonal bag limit of 15 birds, New Hampshire with 25, and North Carolina with 30.

But there's something about *Bonasa* that seems to inspire some members of the grouse-gunning guild to set a self-imposed seasonal limit. During the bonanza years of the 1950s, 10 birds a season seemed a reasonable limit to me. But with more people and fewer birds in my coverts, I've cut my limit to four grouse a season, a limit that is becoming more academic each year.

If I achieve my limit before the end of the season, I still go afield. Instead of my shotgun, I carry a walking stick. On one such trip I met a couple of hunters. In the course of the usual jawboning, I had to explain why I was in the woods without a gun. As we parted, I glanced back and caught one of the hunters in the act of making circular motions with his finger at the side of his forehead.

A law continues to be a necessary tool of management. Because it regulates when a hunter can hunt, the methods he can use, and the amount of game he can take, the law is certainly one of the most effective management tools.

Also the law is democratic in that it applies to all hunters, equally. A statewide bag limit on grouse, for example, is a fair, across-the-board method of regulating the harvesting of the annual crop.

From a biological point of view, though, and especially taking into account grouse cycles, it makes more scientific sense if bag limits are adjusted to smaller geographical units and determined by local scarcity or abundance. Alaska and British Columbia, for example, have established a zoning system and fix bag limits accordingly. Oregon and New York follow a similar approach in setting grouse-hunting seasons.

Although we can date conservation laws from Biblical times, predator control has an even longer history.

When the Pleistocene man, who hunted to survive, watched a wolf snatch his next meal, he invented ways to eliminate his competition. When the scene shifted to North America, and the ruffed grouse was the quarry, I imagine the Eskimo or the Indian were as exasperated as the modern hunter who blows his stack when another kind of hunter—furred or feathered, finned or winged—moves in ahead of him.

Predators are no longer a threat to a hunter's survival, but they are a daily threat to the ruffed grouse throughout its life. Of 1411 nests checked during the New York State Ruffed Grouse Investigation, 553 were broken up by predators. The chief offenders were the fox, weasel, and great horned owl. The fox and weasel are chiefly the nest robbers, and the owl preys on the grouse itself.

Practicing its own kind of foxy conservation, a fox may take some eggs from a grouse nest and leave the rest. Then it may return.

Foxes have a peculiar habit of taking a few eggs from a nest and leaving the remainder. Sometimes a fox will visit the same nest a second time, but again will take a few and leave a few, practicing its own foxy kind of conservation.

During the brooding period, the principal predators of grouse chicks are the hawks and the fox, followed by the great horned owl, crows, and weasels.

In the case of adult grouse, the hawks, chiefly goshawk and Cooper's hawk, and, again, the great horned owl, account for about 75 percent of the ruffed grouse destroyed. The fox is a prominent predator in all of the grouse's life stages.

Predator control, especially when beefed up with bounties, was for years a popular program of game departments and even more popular with sportsmen.

Since the days of Henry VIII, bounties have been put on dozens of critters: from weasels to wildcats, buzzards to bullfinch, and ringtails to ravens.

But the bounty program is full of flaws. Often an animal presented for payment would have been taken by hunters or trappers anyway. Or a farmer, protecting his investment, will shoot the fox that raids his hen house regardless of the cash rewards.

And since 1683, when William Penn put a bounty on wolves, accomplished bounty sharks know all the tricks of the trade. Animals taken in a nonbounty county by today's tricksters show up in a county that pays a bounty. Where states or counties have different marking systems, one animal can often be parlayed into several payments: a slit nose can be presented in one place, a punched ear in another, and a tail in another.

In evaluating predator control as a tool of grouse management, wildlife biologists have concluded that such control cannot be depended upon to increase grouse abundance.

Another related factor game managers take into account is the role of "buffer" species—animals that may serve as staple foods for predators, taking some of the pressure off the game species.

Among the predators that reduce the ruffed grouse's survival odds are the weasel, the great horned owl, the fox, and the hawks—chiefly the goshawk and Cooper's hawk.

Grouse hunters will be relieved to know that in no instance do ruffed grouse serve as the staple food of any predator. Such species as mice, shrews, squirrels, varying hare, and cottontail rabbit are the ''buffers'' that sometimes keep predators from making excessive inroads on grouse populations.

Overriding all considerations is the accepted principle that predators are part of the checks and balances that nature has for keeping a species population within the carrying capacity of a covert.

And even in the best coverts, which would seemingly support many more birds, the social tolerance of the ruffed grouse for its own kind rarely allows more than one adult bird per four acres.

Wildlife refuges were an early form of game management.

Wildlife refuges, like predator control, were an early form of game management. In England, Henry VIII—how that name keeps bobbing up in the history of hunting for sport—set up Britain's first refuge in 1536 by closing an area near Westminster Palace to the shooting of partridges, pheasants, and herons. It has been hinted, however, that this was a bit of royal hanky-panky to improve his own hunting.

England's James I gets the credit for being the first to set aside a refuge for the benefit of game instead of for the benefit of the hunter. During James' reign in the early 1600s, an act was passed establishing a kind of refuge—protected areas in which it was illegal to discharge a gun within 600 paces of a heronry.

A wildlife refuge has almost as many aliases as the ruffed grouse. A park often serves as a refuge—like Yellowstone, where deer, elk, bears, and other animals are free to roam unmolested. Sometimes a refuge is called a reserve, bringing up images of African safaris. Or a refuge may be labeled a preserve. In recent years, though, the term preserve is more likely to refer to just the opposite—a commercial shooting establishment.

To modern game managers, a refuge is an area closed to hunting and with recognizable boundaries. The boundaries may be natural, like a stream, or man-made, like a logging road or fencing. As part of a game-management plan, this kind of refuge adjoins an open hunting area environmentally favorable for the managed species. The expectation is that excess population in the refuge section will be attracted to the adjoining hunting area, thereby improving the shooting.

A rare chance to make a practical assessment in the field occurred during the New York State Ruffed Grouse Investigation.

The Pharsalia Game Refuge in central New York had been established five years before the New York State Ruffed Grouse Investigation got under way, and the adjoining Chenango Public Hunting Grounds Area had been opened up one year before.

The ruffed grouse was the principal game species in the two locales. Both areas were about the same size. A comparison of the composition, amount, and interspersion of cover types revealed no important qualitative differences. Hunting pressure was considered average on the public hunting area.

A census was made for three successive winters. Flushes, tracks, droppings, and grouse kills provided the basis for estimating grouse populations.

SUMMARY OF CENSUS STUDY

	First Year		Second Year		Third Year	
Estimated Grouse Populations	Refuge	Hunting Grounds	Refuge	Hunting Grounds	Refuge	Hunting Grounds
	166	252	134	135	117	163

While the Hunting Grounds showed a modest increase in the third year over the second, the grouse population was considerably less than in the first year of the study. The refuge showed a steady decline in both the second and third years.

Frank Edminster,[18] who supervised the study, noted: ". . . instead of producing a greater supply of grouse, [the refuge] actually had fewer birds than the check area in two of the three years. . . . while analysis of the effect of small differences in the areas may serve to explain some of the variations in grouse numbers, the fact still remains that the protection afforded by the refuge . . . did not serve to enlarge the crop of grouse."

Conceivably, a refuge might serve to prevent extermination. But *Bonasa* apparently derives little benefit from refuge protection—its population fluctuations follow its own inner timetable.

As with refuges, predator control, and game laws, the artificial propagation of gamebirds has a long history as a management measure. From the beginning there have been two procedures: the natural method under the hen, and the artificial incubator-brooder method.

The incubator is far from being a modern invention. Six thousand years ago, Egyptians used incubators modeled in clay to hatch out eggs of the semitame fowl wandering around their dooryards.

British gamekeepers have long spurned the incubator-brooder method. And when the early colonists encountered that

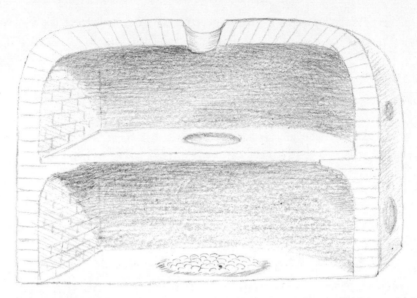

This cross-section view reveals the interior of an incubator fashioned of clay 6,000 years ago by the Egyptians to hatch fowl eggs.

native American, the ruffed grouse, they carried on the British tradition, using the mother-hen method in their attempts to propagate the bird.

Collecting eggs from wild nests, farmers tried to hatch them under chickens, usually bantam hens. But the ruffed grouse, with its American spirit of independence, has always resisted man's efforts to raise it in captivity.

John Bartram,[7] the Pennsylvania patron of the ruffed grouse responsible for helping to get *Bonasa* christened in the zoological world, wrote in 1750:

"Many have attempted to raise young ones and to tame them. When hatched under a hen, they escape into the woods where either they find means to subsist, or perish."

Over 150 years of trials with the natural method only confirmed Bartram's conclusions. Around 1900, finally convinced that the bantam-hen method was unreliable, some game breeders turned to the incubator-brooder system with its improved control of the propagation procedure.

The real problem of raising ruffed grouse in captivity, however, proved to be the heavy mortalities, beginning with the chick stage.

Here again, Dr. Arthur Allen of Cornell University, in his efforts to solve this problem, made a significant contribution. Taking advantage of the gains made in poultry science, Dr. Allen used the most up-to-date incubators and brooders and put together diets based on scientifically compounded formulas. And, noting the success in rearing turkeys and chickens on wire, he began to raise ruffed grouse on wire. When the birds were raised on wire, many of the maladies plaguing grouse reared by the natural-cover method were brought under control.

Gardiner Bump[10] studied under Dr. Allen. When Bump became leader of the New York State Ruffed Grouse Investigation, he started a program of raising grouse on wire at the Delmar Research Center. There, eleven generations of birds were raised whose feet never touched the ground!

Having a supply of ruffed grouse available for stocking coverts was the dream of the old-school game breeders. And today it's a dream of the new breed of game managers: birds to liberate in new coverts, or in old coverts during the low period of cycles; birds to restore stocks reduced by severe weather conditions; birds to replenish populations diminished by disease, predators, or "overshooting."

As a result of Allen's and Bump's work, it is now possible to rear a limited number of ruffed grouse, making direct-observation research feasible. An example is the outstanding studies carried on at the Delmar Research Center, which have added so much to our knowledge of the ruffed grouse's life-style. But raising a large number of birds on a production basis is apparently not a possibility in the near future.

One big drawback is the nature of the grouse. Some gamebirds, such as pheasants and quail, can be fooled into laying more than a conventional clutch by removing eggs as they are laid. Pheasant hens have laid 104 fertile eggs; bobwhite-quail hens, as many as 128. But the ruffed grouse is too smart to be conned by this deceptive practice. The average complement of eggs at the Research Center was from 15 to 20—just a few more than the average clutch in the wild. It's just another example of the grouse's innate resistance to an artificial existence as opposed to a natural way of life.

Furthermore, pen-raised ruffed grouse, lacking the wild spirit of the woodland bird, do not seem to thrive—or even survive—when stocked in a natural environment.

Michigan, for example, has been successful in establishing populations of ruffed grouse in several of its Great Lakes islands with trapped wild stock. However, in the one case where pen-raised birds were used—Hog Island in Lake Michigan—the introduction was a failure, even though the grouse came from the eggs of wild birds.

Summing up the role of artificial propagation as a tool of game management, L. Dale Fay,[23] Michigan Department of Conservation, who has raised grouse for experimental stocking in recent years, stated: "Indiscriminate or large-scale stocking is not warranted in present-day grouse management. Useful purposes can be served, however, through raising and maintaining grouse in captivity for research and stocking in special situations."

To a legion of grouse hunters, artificial propagation's lack of success is a blessing in disguise. A pen-raised version of the ruffed grouse, without its natural wiliness, would take away much of the mystique and most of the joy of hunting such a magnificently wild creature.

More and more, today's game manager is directing his work toward improvement of the environment as the most effective tool of grouse management. Wildlife biologists are now convinced that if a grouse covert is endowed with a suitable habitat, nature will generally fill it to its carrying capacity.

Over much of the ruffed grouse's range, its habitat is on private land, where work by state agencies is limited. But the approach toward habitat improvement is undergoing a philosophical change in the higher levels of wildlife administration.

In New York, for instance, Herbert Doig, Assistant Commis-

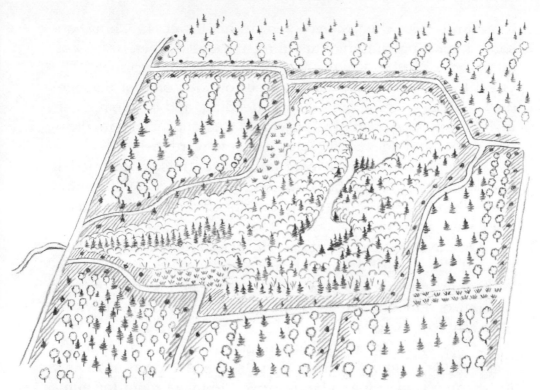

Improvement of the environment gets major emphasis from today's game managers as a tool of grouse management.

sioner for Natural Resources, states: "The trend is toward decentralization. There's a growing emphasis on the home-rule concept and citizen participation. Today's training of wildlife biologists reflects this shift. The new crop comes to us versed in the social implications of land use, along with the traditional, technical training for which there will always be a need and a place."

Since practical habitat improvement is the kind of grouse management work particularly suited to participation by sportsmen, it is a place where grouse hunters can make a meaningful contribution. Here sportsmen's organizations are stepping in to lend a helping hand.

Environmental control, like the other tools of game management, is not a recent development. Aldo Leopold traced it back to around 1300 when Marco Polo, in his travels in China, observed food patches planted for partridges, pheasants, and quails on the Kublai Khan's hunting estate at Changanoor. "The Great Khan" had a surprisingly well-rounded plan of management: refuges, a program of winter feeding, and a code regulating the sport. Apparently poaching was a problem in those times, too, and keepers doubled as game wardens.

In England, the first environmental controls were aimed at ending destructive practices. In 1694, for instance, William and Mary, Britain's only joint rulers, prohibited the burning of nesting cover in the spring.

On the European continent, practices seemed to lean more toward the benefit of the hunter than the benefit of game. Among accepted practices was the clearing and baiting of areas in front of shooting blinds to bring deer and wild boar within easy range of the guns.

In America, the early New England settlers broke up the solid stands of timber. To the colonists, the forest was an enemy to be conquered, a foe to be destroyed to make room for home sites and crop fields.

Impressed by the large number of grouse drawn to the clearings around their buildings, those early Americans believed: "If there are so many partridges around our settlements, how much more plentiful they must be in the deep woods."

But unwittingly they were practicing sound grouse management. The new open spaces, now flooded with sunlight, fostered a luxuriant growth of shrubs and plants that were loaded with food to the grouse's liking. As a result, nearly every clearing triggered a population explosion of birds. For although the ruffed grouse is classified as "forest game" by wildlife managers, they know—as does the newest hunter after a few trips afield— that the deep woods is the poorest place to find birds.

Since New England and the other parts of *Bonasa*'s range remained, basically, an agricultural society for almost two centuries, the habitat of the ruffed grouse also stayed remarkably stable.

The farm woodlot was the key to grouse abundance. Each year, between fall harvest and maple-syrup time, a farmer cut his wood supply for the next year. That custom practically guaranteed a succession of new coverts, pulling in a fresh supply of birds year after year and perpetuating a grouse hunter's paradise.

The rise of a predominantly industrial society has destroyed much of *Bonasa*'s habitat throughout many of the rural areas of the ruffed grouse's range.

At first, the planting of trees, shrubs, and other plants attractive to grouse was an idea that appealed to game managers as an aid in restoring some of the lost habitat.

But during the New York Ruffed Grouse Investigation, Gardiner Bump and Frank Edminster[10] decided: "It is only through experience that one learns of the substantial difficulties lying in the path of establishing good cover by planting. Then the desirability of making the most of existing cover is fully appreciated."

In some situations, however, plantings can be the way to achieve an improved habitat. In Iowa, for example, where disappearance of the ruffed grouse resulted from the clearing of timber and the heavy pasturing of woodlands, reforestation and the establishment of many privately-owned tree farms seem to have swung the habitat balance in favor of ruffed grouse again.

But the old farm woodlot continues to be the basic factor governing grouse populations. And the woodlot principle translates into the creation of clearings as a sound tool of ruffed-grouse management. By varying the location of clearings over a period of time, managers produce a good balance of cover types in both the young and older stages of plant-life succession, providing food and shelter.

Plowing and grazing could be used in rare instances to alter grouse habitat. The plowing of open fields and pastures turns up dormant seeds and makes it easier for windblown seeds to take hold.

An example of sportsmen working to improve the habitat of the bird they love to hunt utilizes the plowing principle. The project is jointly sponsored by the Ruffed Grouse Society of Western New York and the regional office of the New York State Department of Environmental Conservation. A tractor is used to pull a disk harrow over a cleared area, downwind from an aspen stand. The purpose is to find out if breaking up the sod mat by disking will enable the fragile aspen seeds to take hold.

Grazing is a natural method of thinning cover. But if grazing is continued over a long period, it's a sure way of putting a grouse covert into biological bankruptcy.

Killing trees by girdling—removing the bark in a wide cut around the trunk—is another possibility for altering existing cover. However, the method has largely been written off because the dead trees remain standing and continue to partially shade the area and thereby slow up desired plant growth.

Poisoning trees with a chemical works faster than girdling, but here again the trees remain standing for a long time. Testing has shown that sodium arsenite is an effective killing agent, but it often kills desirable surrounding plant life. Apparently the chemical also has a compelling attraction for deer.

From time to time, new and supposedly helpful chemical products come on the market. Virginia recently tested "Dybar." The chemical worked well in most situations as far as creating clearings was concerned. But for some reason Dybar did not fulfill its intended purpose of increasing the grouse population on test areas. Its use was discontinued.

Surprisingly enough, fire has proved to be an effective tool for manipulating grouse habitat. It's often the cheapest way to set back the succession clock. I say it's surprising because of the ever-present danger that fire might get out of control and the potential danger that excessive heat might sterilize the soil by destroying the basic elements.

However, in some recent armchair grouse management, Herb Doig pointed out to me: "A better understanding of fire ecology has revived burning as a management tool for grouse. One of the disadvantages of the past was caused by a 'hot fire.' A drawback largely overcome by burning with a 'cool fire.'"

As Herb explained it, by limiting areas to open fields, which permit a fast burn, and doing the work in the spring when the ground is cool and moist, it is possible to set back plant succession yet preserve the quality of the soil. In fact, the potash residue stimulates the growth of plants and shrubs.

The University of New Hampshire's Institute of Natural and Environmental Resources has conducted workshops to improve the use of fire as a management practice. The Institute found that controlled burning, when used after cutting, prevented or delayed the regeneration of sprout hardwoods and encouraged the growth of aspen and a variety of blackberries, raspberries, clover, and grasses.

Despite the revival of fire as a method of creating clearings, clear-cutting is still the most widely-used technique.

In fact, the main purpose of the Ruffed Grouse Society of Western New York Project is to "utilize tree cutting techniques which will best create the type of forest cover required by the grouse throughout a 12-month period."

Here was a situation where Herb Doig and his staff could lend a helping hand in keeping with the home-rule idea and citizen participation.

Herb's wide range of accomplishments was recognized by the Ruffed Grouse Society in 1976 when the parent organization gave him its "Chief of the Year" award. The honor was earned by his cooperation and assistance and his guidance and counseling. A fitting award for a man who regards the ruffed grouse as his Number 1 gamebird.

And Herb expresses his feelings about grouse hunting: "I can remember every hunt. There's something about grouse hunting that seems to stimulate total recall. The bird itself, the surroundings, and the weather. In your memory, it never rains during the grouse-hunting season."

The old woodlot principle continues to be the cornerstone of sound environmental grouse management.

Connecticut notes that "with the public's renewed interest in wood burning for home heating and a high percentage of the state's forest stands reaching maturity and marketable size, the sales of cordwood and saw logs are booming and the chain saws are buzzing. . . . improvements in grouse habitat should result from these cutting activities."

North Carolina is another good example of the close tie-in between good grouse habitat and cutting operations:

"The ruffed grouse is hunted heavily in the more accessible regions of its range in North Carolina where woodlots are small. . . . The potential for improvement in habitat conditions will depend on market development for short-length hardwood logs for the furniture industry, the use of green wood chips for fuel, and firewood for home heating. Present day trends of these markets are on the upswing and offer some encouragement for the ruffed grouse."

New Hampshire, studying grouse sites through a 20-year period, found that lumbering created 75 percent of the openings.

In Pennsylvania, the outstanding ruffed-grouse state in the East, cutting is important in the overall picture. The Keystone State sums it up:

"Now and in the future, timber harvests will increase as the timber becomes marketable size. With it, I expect the grouse habitat to improve with an attendant increase in the grouse population."

In Minnesota, Michigan, and Wisconsin, aspen dominates grouse habitat. Keeping aspen stands in rotation in the age classes used by grouse helps to keep annual state harvests at the 500,000 level or more.

In Minnesota, where the increasing demand for agricultural crop land operates against pheasants, and more intensive harvesting of forest lands favors grouse, the native ruffed grouse has replaced the introduced ringneck as the most popular game-bird.

Michigan, which has been producing the largest ruffed-grouse annual harvests of any state in recent years, links grouse and deer in its management work:

"Here we are treating intolerant aspen stands by cutting,

burning, herbicide. . . . we average about 28,000 acres a year, and both species have benefited."

The word from Wisconsin: "The majority of timber acres in this state containing significant aspen (and grouse) are receiving cutting treatment adequately enough to maintain good grouse productivity for a long time to come."

The interdependence of management and research shows up in the work underway in the states and provinces.

Minnesota reports: "We have had ruffed-grouse habitat research going on here for quite a few years under the leadership of Gordon Gullion of the University of Minnesota."

Gullion[26] states: "Our research to date indicates that individual cutting blocks should not exceed 10 acres in size and should be sufficiently dispersed so that at least one-quarter of each 40-acre block provides one of the three habitat requirements [brood cover, shelter for wintering and breeding, and wintering-food resource]. . . ."

A grouse-habitat study in New York is underway to see if the aspen-management practices so successful in Michigan, Minnesota, and Wisconsin will be effective in the Northeast. The Ruffed Grouse Society agreed to contribute $10,000 a year over a 10-year period. The project will be in cooperation with the New York State Department of Environmental Conservation; the locale will be the Happy Valley Wildlife Management Area near Syracuse.

More specifically, the study will evaluate the role of aspen as an area habitat factor and the value of conifer stands in coverts where snow-roosting conditions are less favorable than in the northern Great Lakes States and parts of the West.

North Dakota, teaming up with the North Dakota Forest Service and the University of North Dakota, has a double-barreled research project under way in the Turtle Mountains: a radio telemetry study of the ruffed grouse—a study, in line with Gordon Gullion's views, of growth and regeneration of aspen clearcuts.

South Dakota, too, is studying the relationship between

In the grouse research of many areas, the aspen is a significant factor.

ruffed grouse and aspen in the Black Hills. One drawback of cutting aspen has been the lack of a commercial market. Except for its occasional use as firewood, industrial markets for aspen are practically nonexistent. Surprisingly, South Dakota has discovered that aspen chips, when mixed with conventional ingredients such as alfalfa and soybean oil and then pressed into pellets, produce a satisfactory cattle food.

Utah, another state in which aspen is abundant, has started a project to determine the effects of aspen-cutting practices on ruffed grouse.

Some states have special environmental problems. In Tennessee and West Virginia, for instance, strip mining for coal has destroyed large acreages of ruffed-grouse cover.

Tennessee's long-range program, "A Strategic Plan for Tomorrow's Wildlife Resources Management," stresses the need to encourage reclamation of the environment after strip-mining operations, to benefit grouse.

The close relationship between cutting and good grouse hunting strikes home in my own gunning experience. I shot my first grouse in a cutover area.

The setting of that landmark day was Cascade Ridge at the south end of Owasco Lake, one of New York's Finger Lakes.

I could hear the whine of a band saw up ahead as it cut through a log. A portable sawmill was a common way of lumbering in those days, the rig moving on to another site when the surrounding timber had been cut and sawed. Powered by a single-cylinder gasoline engine, these "one-lungers" had starting strokes and a rhythmic chug that had an irresistible fascination for grouse. The sound, which resembled the drumming of a ruffed grouse, perhaps drew birds in to investigate.

As I moved ahead, the roar of a flush drowned out the sounds of the sawmill. Not one, but three birds thundered up. To see three grouse in the clear at one time was an unsettling experience for a bird hunter who had yet to shoot his first grouse.

I threw the gun to my shoulder, holding, I thought, on the lead bird. To my astonishment the third grouse in line dropped. I sprinted for the spot and grabbed the bird as its wings gave a final flap.

As I looked at the beautiful bird in my hand, I was totally unprepared for the emotional chain reaction that followed. First, surprise at finally getting in a telling shot, followed immediately by the thrill of success. A moment later, I choked up with feelings of remorse. But this reaction, too, was short-lived. The lure of the hunt—deeply rooted in man since the Pleistocene, when it was his way of life—drew me on, eager for a repetition.

Bonasa's performance reflects its remarkable vitality—a vitality that has helped it contend with a declining environment. But the thought, effort, and know-how that go into today's game management make a real contribution to the improvement of that habitat. Because of such help, the ruffed grouse and man may continue to live in harmonious coexistence.

But the coverts of the ruffed grouse—even under the most successful management—are more than trees, shrubs, brush, and clearings. A well-managed covert, harboring a full quota of grouse, is a place where encounters can become adventures. A place, too, which often becomes a haven that refreshes the spirit—the ultimate environment for the hunter.

9
Grouse-Gunning Gear

The action-packed drama the gallant grouse brings to the sport, and an autumn covert's poetic imagery, can make a hunter forget about the practical side of grouse hunting.

When you anticipate the excitement to come, it's natural just to grab a gun, jump into the car, and take off. But sooner or later, such a casual approach will spoil the hunt. You'll be overgunned or undergunned; you'll develop a throbbing ache between your

The right gun and other gear can add greatly to your enjoyment of grouse hunting.

shoulders from a badly-fitted hunting coat; you'll get overheated with clothes too heavy or chilled with garb too light; you'll hobble home with blistered feet from poor-fitting boots; you'll get "twigged" without the protection of shooting glasses; you'll wander in circles through the woods for lack of a compass; or you'll have trouble making it back to the car for lack of a chocolate bar.

In getting prepared for action, your primary piece of equipment, of course, is the gun. After you have had enough shooting experience to know the kind of gun you want, it pays to buy the best you can afford. Or perhaps more than you can afford. A good gun, with reasonable care, will last a lifetime. And it will be a lifetime reward, adding depth to that special relationship between a man and his gun.

In the days I was cutting my gunning teeth, I had a recurrent dream in which my cash-flow problems would improve to the point of my being able to invest in a Purdey or one of the other shotguns made by artisans who served under Joseph Manton, the gunsmith who fathered the art in England.

Many of Manton's apprentices set up their own shops—a gunning tale of two cities. Both London and Birmingham became corporate paradises and, for well over a century, have produced a stunning galaxy of famous shotguns: Purdey, Boss, Holland and Holland, Westley Richards, Webley and Scott, and others, disproving the dictum there is room at the top for only one.

But no grouse hunter is underprivileged who owns a good American gun. Guns with a prestigious history date from the time Baker, Fox, Ithaca, Lefever, Parker, Remington, Smith, Winchester, and others designed shotguns in the classic side-by-side model—versions of British counterparts, happily endowed with the same authoritative lock-stock-and-barrel trinity.

Although my dream of owning a Purdey never came true, I was lucky enough to acquire, early in the game, a gun that has been the perfect grouse gun through all my grouse-gunning days. A gun with a sweet feel, it comes up quickly and swings smoothly in tracking a fast-flying bird.

I found it in a country hardware store in Weedsport, New York. That town is on the fringes of what is now the Montezuma National Wildlife Refuge and became famous as the home of the Stevens decoy factory, in business from 1865 to 1910. Stevens's decoys, although machine-made, were a superior product then and are a collectors' item now.

As I stepped inside the country hardware store, my eye—attracted as when a pretty woman enters the room—went right to the gun, one of a dozen or so on a rack.

Putting it to my shoulder, I lined up imaginary grouse, quartering to the left and then to the right. Gun specifications such as comb, heel, pitch, and drop were vague terms to me at that stage of the game, but I was taken with the way the gun came up and swung into position.

In my make-believe covert, I was making shots I've never been able to duplicate in the real gunning world. I held the gun out at arm's length to admire its clean lines. It was love at first sight.

All this did not go unnoticed by the storekeeper.

"Nice little gun, that one," he said as he approached. "It's an Ithaca. Field grade, 20-gauge. And notice those 'snails' ears,'" he added, pointing to the two little knobs on the breech, which indicate whether or not the gun is cocked and ready for action.

"How is it bored?" I asked, trying to sound knowledgeable.

"Right barrel modified, and left, full choke."

My knowledge of shotgun lore exhausted, I moved into the real target area. "How much?"

"Forty dollars."

Again my face telegraphed my thoughts.

"I know," he agreed, "that's a pretty stiff price for these depression times. But that gun has been in the rack for over a year now. Our country trade goes for 12-gauge guns. You can have it for what it cost me."

Several payments later, the gun was mine.

And the little Ithaca still goes with me on every grouse hunt. No, I'll have to amend that. Leo Martin, long associated with the late lamented Abercrombie & Fitch Co. in New York City, fixed me up with a used 12-gauge L. C. Smith. Although I use it mostly in the duck blind, it also plays a role in my grouse hunting. On the principle of a baseball player who swings a couple of bats before stepping up to the plate, I take "Elsie"—alias for an L. C. Smith—with me on my first two or three hunts of the season. When I switch back to the Ithaca, it feels, by contrast, much lighter and swings much faster.

Most of us learn about guns by trial and error. A good short-cut would be to talk with Leo Martin.

Leo was with Abercrombie & Fitch for 45 years and headed up its Gun Department until the day the sporting world was shocked to learn that the 85-year-old firm had gone into bankruptcy.

A tribute to Leo's expertise was the Leo Martin Gun Room where potentates from the Middle East and Texas oil millionaires talked of Purdey, Boss, and Holland & Holland as if dollar bills were No. 6 shot. But I have no doubt that if a kid from Punkin Crick, interested in a rimfire .22, wandered into the store by chance, Leo would have made him feel like an honored customer.

During Leo's years as impresario of the Gun Room, his counsel was sought by hundreds of grouse hunters. And they were counseled well because of Leo's experience with and admiration for the ruffed grouse.

"It's a magnificent bird," Leo told me, with the fervor of a clan member. "A real challenge, too. When you have to work so hard, you value the quarry more."

Leo, like me, is wedded to the classic double. I asked him for his thoughts on a grouse gun: "For myself, the grouse is something special, so I want a gun that is something special. A gun that moves readily, mounts quickly, and swings fast. The Winchester 21 suits me just fine.

"My choice," he said, "is a light 12-gauge, weighing about 6¾ pounds, with 26-inch barrels—bored improved cylinder and modified.

"But that's just a personal preference," Leo emphasized. "For the average grouse hunter, I recommend a lightweight 12-gauge with 28-inch barrels, right barrel modified and the left, full choke."

Such a gun, of course, is a stock model of almost every maker: a gun with a 1½-inch drop at the comb, a 2½-inch drop at the heel, and a 14-inch pull. As for the length of pull, Leo believes a short stock makes a gun fit tighter to the shoulder. "The stock should be just long enough so, on the recoil, your thumb doesn't hit your nose."

The production-line gun is made to fit the average shooter. It does not have the fit or elegance of a custom-made Purdey, but it moves readily, and most gunners soon adapt to it.

"Suppose," I asked, "you had a customer with a build like a linebacker?"

"Surprisingly enough, we could often fix him up with a standard model," Leo said. "Usually it's those long arms that make the problem. The standard 14-inch pull would cramp his arm so he couldn't get his cheek on the stock in the right position to line up the target. Often, lengthening the stock with an over-sized recoil pad was an inexpensive answer to the problem."

When fitted properly, a custom-made gun can be a joy for-ever. But production-line guns are pretty darned good, too. A good example is my steadfast Ithaca.

When I was at Cornell getting my training in conservation, my trail crossed that of Lou Smith, president of Ithaca Gun Company. A brother of L. C. Smith, founder of the L. C. Smith Gun Company, Lou was another member of Thomas Smyth's "staff." Along with Dr. Allen and others, he collected specimens for Tommy's master's and doctor's theses on the food of *Bonasa*. A case of Smith helping Smyth.

Single-trigger double guns were beginning to come into fashion. I deluded myself into thinking that if my production-line Ithaca had a single trigger, I would be the fastest gun in the coverts.

When I talked to Lou Smith about converting the Ithaca to a single trigger, he tried to discourage me.

"Yes, we could convert your gun into a single trigger but, being nonselective, you would always have to fire the modified right barrel first. That takes away the great advantage of a two-barreled gun. If a grouse flushes forty yards out, the left choke barrel is your best bet, but with the single trigger you have to fire the modified barrel first.

"Another thing, with a double-barreled, single trigger," Lou continued, "if you miss the first shot, you have a tendency to press the trigger immediately without correcting the aim. With a two-trigger gun, if you miss on the first shot, your natural instinct is to readjust the aim while your finger is moving back to the other trigger. I know a British shooter who seldom misses, but when he does, he purposely drops the gun from his shoulder and remounts to keep from making the same mistake again."

In my case, I'm sure Lou knew it was the gunner that needed improving, not the gun. But seeing my heart was set on a single trigger, he added, "O.K. Bring the gun in and we'll have it changed."

Now, with 20/20 hindsight, I wish I had taken Lou's advice. Just as he tried to tell me, I find it all too easy, with a single trigger, to pull it twice too quickly—and all too easy to miss twice. And many times I have flushed a bird that I might have downed if I could have fired the choke barrel first.

For grouse hunting, Lou, like Leo Martin, recommended a lightweight 12-gauge gun for its heftier load and wider pattern.

"Always remember," Lou once told me, "a 12-gauge gun will do everything a 20-gauge will do. And do it better."

In spite of the recommendation of Leo and Lou, I'm still wedded to my 20-gauge Ithaca.

The theoretically proper grouse load is not always the one that works best in practice.

But even the most carefully selected gun can't live up to its potential if it doesn't have the proper load for the quarry you're hunting.

When I started grouse hunting, I operated on the principle that the heavier the load was, the better. But not only did these high-base loads fail to improve my score, but also the jolt of the recoil gave me one of the damnedest flinches a gunner was ever cursed with. One time a box of shells contained a dud. In the silence of the resulting misfire, I realized I was jerking the gun skyward, in a reflex action, way off target, with absolutely no follow-through.

To a wingshooter, a flinch is as welcome as a tarantula in his shell pocket. I'm convinced that most flinches develop as the result of using high-base loads. In my own grouse hunting, I know my swing became a little smoother and my follow-through a little better when I changed to lighter loads.

What the proper load is, in theory, is not always the right load, in practice. Lou Smith once told me that every smoothbore made by man or machine will throw a different pattern, even though both gun and shells have been made to the same specifications and tolerances measured in thousandths of an inch.

Fred Etchen,[22] an outstanding shooting instructor who coached his son, Rudy, to be one of the truly greats in the clay-target world, puts this thought even stronger: "It is my opinion that hunters and shooters generally pay too much attention to the choke of their gun and not enough to the size of the shot, the amount of shot, and the powder load."

If you really want to get down to the fine points on gun performance, consider this advice from Lou Smith: "The best check is to test various loads and shot sizes on a pattern sheet.

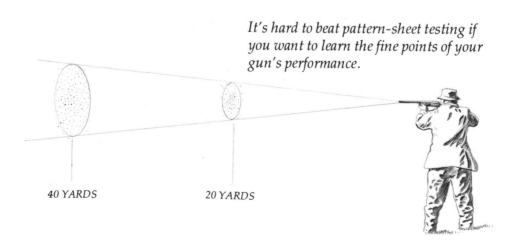

It's hard to beat pattern-sheet testing if you want to learn the fine points of your gun's performance.

40 YARDS   *20 YARDS*

The number of pellets a particular load will put in a 30-inch circle at 40 yards is the standard test."

Lou's suggestion made a lot of sense. I traded some shells with another hunter who also owned a 20-gauge and got a stock-pile of shells in pellet sizes from 5s to 9s in the light load of 2¼ drams of powder. A farmer, who sometimes joined me when I hunted grouse in his woodlot, let me put the pattern sheet on the side of his barn for testing, although he was firmly convinced I was crackers.

After tacking up the first pattern sheet, I measured off 40 yards. It seemed so short, I taped it again. Hard to believe that most grouse shots are taken within that distance.

In the choke barrel, all shot sizes gave good, uniform patterns. In the modified barrel, patterns were satisfactory. But I was surprised to find that 5s made more pellet holes in the 30-inch circle than 6s, even though the load of 5s contained 55 fewer pellets. Pellet-hole counting turned into quite a chore. I was continually losing count. I finally hit upon the obvious idea of marking each hole with an X as I counted it.

In both choke and modified barrels, No. 8s and 9s tested about the same, with a good tight pattern. I decided to go with No. 8s instead of 9s because the slightly heavier 8s maintain better velocity in flight.

Velocity in flight can be an important factor, especially on long shots. Leo Martin, although favoring light powder loads, prefers No. 6s for grouse because the heavier pellets in this load have less tendency to drift in flight than the smaller sizes and retain more wallop at the end of the flight.

Recently when I told Leo about testing the pattern of my Ithaca, he said: "Now that's a really smart thing to do. Actually, it's the best way to find out your gun's potential. Pattern testing is very revealing. The pattern tells you the best size shot to use by showing the pellet distribution. And, by drawing a horizontal and a vertical line through the center of the circle on the pattern sheet, you can find out where your gun is shooting by the position of the pellets. Well-centered, high or low, right or left."

What you learn from pattern testing has carry-over value in a covert. But in the excitement of a flush when a wily grouse is your target, you don't think of the shot pattern. If you're using a load that has tested satisfactorily on a pattern sheet, though, your confidence is bolstered. You know that if you do your job of lining up the bird correctly, the charge will do its job.

I may be the last grouse hunter who used paper-hulled shells. I first saw plastic shells in 1956, spotting them in a sporting-goods store window in—of all places—Chartres, France, just around the corner from the famous Cathedral. I was fascinated because the cases were transparent, showing the load makeup just about as clearly as the cutaway sketches of shells in catalogues.

Plastic shells soon came on the American market, but I never saw any with clear-plastic cases. Plastic shells, because of their waterproof quality, immediately became popular.

Just about the time plastic shells began coming off assembly lines, a dealer, afraid he would be stuck with unwanted paper shells, offered me a bargain in No. 8s that I couldn't turn down.

When stacked, the shells took over most of my gun cabinet. The lady of the house quipped: "Now I know how the term 'ammunition dump' got its name."

In addition to shells loaded with 2¼ drams of powder—a load I had been using—I got several dozen boxes loaded with 2½ drams.

After a lot a field-testing, I now use a 2¼ x ⅞ shell in the right barrel. In the choke barrel goes the heavier load with 2½ drams of powder and a full ounce of shot, giving me a little more firepower on the second shot when I've missed on the first and the bird is rapidly moving out of range.

As Leo Martin noted, the off-the-rack gun serves the average hunter very well. But an off-the-rack hunting coat, in my opinion, does an actual disservice to a grouse hunter.

I'll admit I'm as persnickety as the grouse about some things. To begin with, the material in most hunting coats today is too heavy and too stiff—sheet-iron duck, old-time hunters called it. Even the so-called lightweight hunting coats are lined with the same material as the outside, double layers negating the very purpose of a lightweight garment.

At one time I could walk into almost any sporting-goods store and pick off the rack a good hunting coat, a coat built to do the job. But some time between the two world wars, manufacturers lost the pattern of those wonderful old coats and are now turning out hunting coats styled like "a three-button Brooks Brothers suit in which to commute."

Captain Paul Curtis,[13] a leading gun editor in the earlier part of the century, declared: "A shooting jacket should be made with more care than a dinner jacket."

If I can ever find a grouse-hunting tailor to whom my finicky ways make sense, my ideal hunting coat will be made of the lightest fabric I can get, yet strong enough—something like the material used in the sails of America's Cup defenders—to withstand constant confrontations with brush, briers and brambles. Every grouse hunter worthy of the name must investigate thick cover time after time during a day's hunt.

Leo and I are on the same wavelength on most grouse-gunning gear, including lightweight hunting coats.

"In fact," Leo said, "I find I go afield more and more in my trapshooting jacket. It's light, easy on the shoulders, and the pleats permit easy action. And so darned comfortable, I never think of what I'm wearing."

When wearing a lightweight jacket, a hunter can maintain his thermal equilibrium by varying what he wears underneath: on Indian-Summer days, a T shirt; on cooler days, a wool shirt; and on the coldest days, longjohns or, better yet, thermal or fishnet underwear.

My grouse-hunting coat will be not only designed but also engineered. Although the material will be virtually weightless, it will be sewed to web straps so that it will hang like a rucksack, all the weight resting squarely on the shoulders. The sleeves will have a gusset at the armpit so I'm not lifting the weight of a couple dozen shells every time I raise the gun to my shoulder;

and an action pleat in the back of the jacket at the shoulder seam so there's no bind when I swing on a crossing bird.

Other touches will be a crossover throat latch to snug up when a stiff north wind adds to the chill factor, and a fly front to keep buttons from snagging in the brush.

For freedom of movement, the buttons will be positioned high enough so one will not pop when I step over a log or hunker down under a pine tree for a momentary breather during an icy November rain.

There will be no game pocket. Instead, a shoulder button will hold a leather-thong game carrier. That idea is one I got from Old Ed, the market hunter.

"Stuffin' a warm bird in the pocket of a huntin' coat is a sure way to ruin the meat of a pa'tridge," he told me. "Let 'em cool out first. Our birds always brought top prices. They was payin' us three dollars a brace just before nineteen 'leven when the law put a stop to market huntin'."

Since I usually carry a lunch, the coat will have a detachable bag that buttons to the back, placed where it will fit in the small of my back, instead of banging against my fanny as it does in the game pocket of today's off-the-rack coat. After lunch, the bag will be folded up and tucked away in a side pocket.

Speaking of pockets, the fewer and shallower, the better. There was a time when I thought a hunting coat could never have enough pockets, nor were they ever large enough. But a form of Parkinson's Law evolves: the more pockets you have and the bigger they are, the more stuff you carry.

It doesn't matter when a hunter starts out, but after pushing through tough grouse cover for several hours, he will be tempted to empty every pocket. No wonder Caesar's legions called their equipment *impedimenta*.

Many grouse hunters prefer the hunting vest. Most of these sleeveless garments are just an assemblage of pockets.

"I really can't understand why anyone would prefer a vest," Leo Martin commented, "considering the kind of cover a grouse hunter is always getting into."

I bought a hunting vest when they first came on the market, but a couple of trial runs convinced me it was not for my kind of grouse hunting. Twigs and branches were continually catching at the armholes. Once I was thrown off balance just as I pushed off the safety and pulled the trigger. A wild shot into the brush scared hell out of me, thinking what might have happened if I had been hunting with a companion.

If I have overreacted to modern hunting coats and vests, I do an about-face when it comes to the hunting pants of today. Over the years, pants have improved tremendously in both cut and material.

Of all the garb that hunters wear, pants seem to bring out the rugged individualist more than any other garment. John James Audubon, in 1804, startled the people of Penns Woods—and probably the forest animals—by going afield in satin knee breeches. One of my early hunting companions wore golfer's plus fours with western-style canvas chaps over them. The farmer, whose barn I used for testing shell patterns, wore his bib overalls when he joined me in a hunt.

Still another comrade wore riding britches. They struck my fancy, and I bought a pair made of twill and had a cobbler sew a horsehide facing on the front. Their flamboyant flare, according to my style-conscious wife, made me look like a Ringling Brothers ringmaster.

When my riding britches finally wore out, the trouser type of pants with a canvas-duck facing was on the market. This type of pants wears well and has been standard equipment in my hunting ever since.

But no matter how tough a hunting garment is, it will eventually lose out to grouse cover. I remember well the demise of my last hunting pants. I was wading through a jungle of briers, trying to push out a particularly recalcitrant bird, when the outseam of one leg opened up from cuff to belt.

Halfway through the patch and at the point of no return, I had to keep going. Every step through thorny cover was torture. In time, I discovered that by turning sideways, I could use my good pant leg to run interference for the torn one. The stubborn grouse recognized this as a good time to take off. If offered me an easy crossing shot to the left and well within range, but my lee tack permitted no follow-through and I waffled with both barrels.

Although my canvas-faced bush pants continue to be my usual favorites, I abandon them when I expect to hunt in thornapple country. I put on a pant with a vinyl facing. Vinyl, in addition to protecting against bull briers, is lighter than leather and sheds water like a duck's back. To make it easier to step over logs, the pants are "stagged"—shortened so the bottom of the leg comes a few inches above the ankle, but still below the boot top.

Since a grouse hunt is a strenuous walking sport from start to finish, the grouse hunter's boot is almost as important as the grouse hunter's gun.

The boot should be tough for walking through rocky pastures and pushing through blackberry tangles. It should have good traction for climbing rocky ridges and be waterproof for slogging through swamps. Above all, the boot should be pliable for easiness afoot and lightweight so feet don't begin to drag early in the hunt. The true test of being perfectly shod in a grouse covert is to be completely unaware of wearing boots.

When I started hunting grouse, a favorite locale was Featherbed Swamp, part of the Montezuma Marsh archipelago in central New York. Between little islands of coverts, there was a lot of sloshing through terrain covered with a couple of inches of water. Like my companions, I wore knee-high rubber boots, the

If you "stag" your pants legs, you'll have less trouble stepping over logs.

kind that are the trademark of the French-Canadian habitant. My riding britches, laced snugly below the knee, left a lot of open space at the top of the boot, and that space let in a lot of water. Also twigs, thorns, briers, and burrs.

I changed from Lucky Pierre's boot to a laced boot with rubber bottom and leather top. It was the Maine Hunting Shoe—never called boot—which brought renown and riches to Leon Leonwood Bean.

This general type of footwear, now made by several firms, is the best all-purpose boot for grouse hunting. A dry boot. I always thought that worrying about wet feet was sissy stuff. But now reliable studies have shown that wet feet, by siphoning off body heat, dangerously lowers body temperature and can induce hypothermia.

But in my hill-country grouse coverts, I seldom need a waterproof boot. There I like the all-leather moccasin-type boot best of all, and I splurged on a pair of Russell Bird Shooters.

The Bird Shooters are holding up well after years of hard hunting. I'm especially partial to the more closely spaced eyelets over the instep, which not only give good ankle support but also help to protect the tongue from briers. And the beveled heel slides easily over woodland debris, cutting down on the inevitable stumble-bumbling that goes with grouse hunting.

*The right socks help the grouse hunter
avoid blisters and bone bruises.*

The advantages of the best-fitting boots can be spoiled by poor-fitting socks. To avoid blisters and bone bruises, a grouse hunter needs plenty of cushion underfoot.

For many years, I thought more was better and wore three pairs of socks with my hunting boots (also with fishing waders). A few years ago, however, I arrived at streamside with only two pairs. I immediately noticed I could wiggle my toes inside the waders, a freedom that improved my footing on the treacherous stream bottom.

Now, on the comparably rough terrain of a grouse covert, I'm a confirmed advocate of the two-pairs-of-socks school: first a pair of the lightest-weight white cotton; over those, a pair of the heaviest wool hunting socks. An added twist is to turn both pairs of socks inside out so that the seam ridges won't chafe the foot—another little trick I learned from Old Ed.

Headgear completely suitable for grouse hunting is yet to be designed. The ageless Jones hat, so good in a duck blind, is as appropriate in a grouse covert as a stovepipe hat. It will be on the ground as much as on your head. A cap seems to be the best bet. Many grouse hunters wear a baseball cap.

Years ago, L. L. Bean listed a bird-hunting cap of light-weight duck in olive drab. Although it makes me look more like a railroad engineer than a grouse hunter, it's well constructed— with a leather sweatband and a leather outside binding—and still going strong.

A cap's peak not only shades your eyes but also has another advantage: by pulling the peak down over your eyes and closer to your nose, you make your line of vision a narrow slit, reducing the margin-of-error area in lining up a bird.

The visor also provides some eye protection in the brush. But unless you wear shooting glasses, sooner or later a twig is bound to snap back and hit an eye while you're going through thick grouse cover. Not only a painful experience but also one that can actually cause serious injury to an eye—perhaps even a scraped cornea.

Shooting glasses serve two purposes: eye protection, and

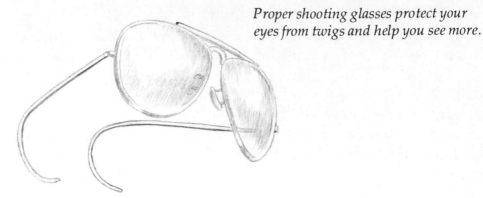

*Proper shooting glasses protect your
eyes from twigs and help you see more.*

better visibility. Some gunners, like many airplane pilots, prefer a gray lens because it feels more comfortable to the eye. But those versed in optics point out the gray version defeats one of the great advantages of shooting glasses—increased illumination. A gray lens favors the spectrum's blues and violets, a condition that tends to make a flying grouse blend into the background.

On the other hand, a yellow filter, as photographers know, creates a sharper image by enhancing contrast. Taking an added tip from the grouse itself, which like all birds noted for their keen vision has a yellow cast to its eye, I prefer shooting glasses with yellow lenses. Toward the end of a gloomy November day, yellow lenses not only define objects more sharply but also make shadowy grouse cover seem flooded with sunlight.

Brier scratches are always a hazard for the grouse hunter. Gloves will keep a hunter from getting his hands scratched, but most grouse hunters like the feel of a bare finger against the trigger and scorn shooting gloves even on the coldest days. The mitten-type of hand protection with a slit across the palm is much too clumsy for grouse hunting.

I've tried many so-called shooting gloves, but they always finished out their service in yard chores. On a trip through Vermont a few years ago, I spotted a pair of splithide deerskin gloves. The moment I tried on a pair, I had a feeling they would be the answer to the problem of shooting gloves.

They were. They keep fingers warm on cold days and dry out softly after getting wet. Their pliability permits a surprisingly sensitive touch with the trigger finger. Even on warm days, when I must make a frontal assault on a brier patch, I slip a glove on my left hand to give protection as I part the bushes while moving through a thorny tangle.

High on the grouse hunter's list of essential equipment is a sharp knife. On warm days, a downed grouse should be field-dressed immediately to preserve the meat. A sharp knife spells the difference between a neat and quick autopsy and a messy job.

At first, I carried a hunting knife in a belt sheath, fancying that it added a Jim Bowie cachet to the image I had of myself as a macho outdoorsman. Too big and heavy, it was limited to chopping off wings and legs. So I resurrected an old pocketknife with carbon-steel blades that keep a scalpel-sharp edge with a minimum of honing—"it's the dull knife that cuts you."

Some gunners make a grouse hunt a no-frills trip. Others pack enough stuff for an expedition into the wilderness. I try not to load up with the countless gunners' gizmos that flood the marketplace and seduce the hunter.

A couple of Band-Aids for the grouse hunter's inevitable cuts and scratches and a few safety pins do not alter my resolve to travel light. It's surprising how many ways a simple safety pin will pinch-hit—like doing the work of a popped button or mending a three-cornered tear after barbed wire exacts its toll.

A few pieces of chocolate are not a luxury; they're a necessity as an energy booster for the long trek back to headquarters. As long ago as 1519, Hernando Cortes, Spanish conquistador, recording the exploration of Mexico, discovered the value of chocolate: ". . . it gives you strength to march all day long."

And, let's hope, to march in the right direction. One of the smallest but most important pieces of equipment is a compass. Many hunters think a compass is essential only for hunting in wilderness areas. But even in familiar territory, there are times you need a compass to keep you on the right track.

I have a vivid recollection of hunting a home covert when a cotton-wool ground fog suddenly settled in—so thick I could barely see beyond the end of the gun barrel. Although only a couple of gunshots from home, I wandered around in an eerie, strange world for several hours. Finally, I came upon a woods path I recognized. Luckily, just before dark.

Getting lost in familiar grouse cover may seem like a far-fetched idea, but painful experience has proved it can happen. Be ready with a compass and other survival essentials.

From then on, I have always carried a compass. In fact, I carry two: one is a vintage Marble pin-on, firmly sewed on for added insurance under the flap of the breast pocket of my hunting jacket; the other is part of a combination gadget—a waterproof matchbox with a compass built into one end and a whistle in the other. The matchbox is kept filled with wooden matches that are never used except in an emergency. Be sure to glue a piece of striker strip inside the lid.

In strange territory, a U.S. Geological Survey topographic map is also helpful, especially when used with a compass. Indeed, it is foolhardy to go afield without one. It shows contours and identifiable landmarks such as roads and ridges, trails, swamps, and streams. Even the inexperienced outdoorsman can easily learn to use such a map for locating his general—and often his exact—position.

But the truly dedicated grouse hunter goes afield with more than outer, man-made trappings; he sets out equipped with inner senses sharpened for the challenges to come.

I am grateful for that inner compass that first led me to the coverts of the ruffed grouse. Coverts where every hunt leads to new rewards: a lone grouse skyrocketing out of a laurel patch; a late-season brood feeding under a wild apple tree; two cock grouse on the bend of a logging road, sparring in gentlemanly fashion for territorial rights. Unforgettable vignettes of the grouse's world.

10

Gunning for Grouse

A sudden whir of wings, a ruffed grouse takes off, exploding almost from under your feet. There is nothing but air between you and the fast-flying bird framed in the sky. This is the wingshooter's moment of truth.

Unnerved, you fire the first barrel too soon. Concentration broken, confidence shattered, you try to settle down, becoming too deliberate. Aiming instead of pointing, you fire the second barrel too late.

A grouse hunter working a piece of cover constantly expects a flush. Yet, when the flush does come, he is invariably startled. It's the exuberant burst of *Bonasa*'s takeoff that generates the firing-too-soon-firing-too-late syndrome.

Every grouse gunner faces the dilemma of trying, despite the flaws in his shooting, to overcome the incredible wiliness of the bird. All hunters are equal before grouse, for it's not the hunter, but the grouse that dominates the hunt. *Bonasa* has an unending repertoire of frustrating tactics: the startling flush; the instinctive flight behind the nearest tree or bush or into impenetrable cover; the sudden, bewildering change of elevation or direction of its flight; sitting tight so you pass by; or flushing far ahead, maddeningly out of range.

Desire is seldom destiny in ruffed-grouse shooting. *Bonasa umbellus* can outwit not only the tyro but often also the seasoned shooter. Even a virtuoso, like Old Ed, a third-generation market hunter who seldom failed to read a shot correctly, was helpless when a bird suddenly slipped out of sight before he could get the gun to his shoulder.

"You can't hit what you can't see. But when a pa'tridge is in the open," he contended, "hittin' is just as easy as pointin' your finger at the bird."

Actually, the finger-pointing comparison is sound since the gun acts as an extension of the arm. Pointing is not only logical but also is the essence of good wingshooting. With a moving target, a shotgun is not aimed as in rifle shooting, but is pointed.

"When a pa'tridge is in the open," said Old Ed, "hittin' it is just as easy as pointin' your finger at the bird."

Like so many hunters of my generation, I started my shooting with a Daisy air rifle. Plinking at tin cans—a pastime that requires a deliberate aim and a slow, easy press of the trigger—is poor training for grouse shooting. The whole action in grouse shooting must be completed in a split second.

Although I batted left-handed in baseball, it seemed natural to put the Daisy to my right shoulder and close my left eye. I was just following the accepted practice of my peers.

Years later, I read about the "master eye" and gave myself the accepted test: aiming my right index finger at an object 6 feet away, I looked at it with both eyes open; then with just the right eye; then just the left. When I closed my right eye, the object held its position; when I closed my left eye, the object jumped nearly a foot to the left. It was a sad day for me as a right-shouldered shooter to learn that nature had given me a left master eye. In shooting from my right shoulder and sighting with my right eye, I lose the advantage of my dominant left eye.

Gunning editors recommend that the shooter in such a fix learn to shoot from the left shoulder with both eyes open. There's no doubt that two eyes are better than one in wingshooting. Binocular sighting sounds easy, but I was never able to make the change with any success. Following the habit of years, I still shoot from the right shoulder and squint my left eye.

A beginning grouse hunter, before he gets too grooved in his gunning ways, would be wise to give binocular sighting a try and shoot from the shoulder on the side of his master eye.

With my master-eye handicap and the bad shooting habits I had picked up on my own, I was lucky to meet Old Ed, who became my grouse-gunning mentor. As a fellow worker doing fish-hatchery chores, in the grouse coverts, or over a few nostril-flaring belts of applejack after a hunt, Old Ed was the kind of companion and teacher most of us look for but never find. And how that man loved pa'tridge hunting, lapping it up like salt-pork gravy, a *specialité* of his cuisine.

But, to me, the measure of the man was the way he adapted to the switch from market hunting to hunting solely for sport.

Old Ed's transformation is a tribute to the ruffed grouse, too. Only an extraordinary gamebird could convert such a no-non-sense market hunter to the sport-hunting persuasion.

How to hit a grouse is not easy to discuss, harder to de-scribe, and even more difficult to distill. But Old Ed had the knack of translating his experience into homespun terms even a beginning grouse hunter could understand.

He was usually easygoing, but those years of market hunt-ing were so ingrained that he changed into a take-charge guy the moment he stepped into a grouse covert.

The outdoor classrooms of what I came to call "Old Ed's School of Pa'tridge Huntin'" bordered the north shore of Oneida Lake in central New York.

An early lesson was a tip on judging the distance of a flushed grouse from the gunner. We had just stepped into a cut-over piece of cover when a bird flushed ahead of us. In a reflex action, I slam-banged the Ithaca to my shoulder.

"Hold it, hold it," Old Ed called over from his side.

Too late. I fired two fast shots. And missed.

"That bird was out of range," Old Ed said with remarkable restraint.

"Yeah, I knew it right after I pulled the trigger. But how can you tell if a bird is in range *before* you pull the trigger?"

"That's somethin' that comes after you've done a lot of shootin'. When I started, Pa told me to think of a baseball field. Say you're standin' at home plate—when a pa'tridge is out by the pitcher's box, is the nearest you want to shoot. Gives the load a chance to open up a bit. Between there and second base is the best time to shoot. I guess your bird was gettin' into center field when you fired."

Eager to improve my image as a pupil, I started off again at a brisk pace.

"Whoa there, whoa," he said, trying to put a check rein on me. "You're like a horse headin' for the barn, and we're just startin'. At this clip, we're goin' by every bird in the county. Let's sit a spell and let things simmer down."

HITTING A RUFFED GROUSE

Where a gunner should hold on a ruffed grouse that flies straight ahead depends on whether the bird is at eye level, below eye level, or above eye level. Each situation is treated here in turn.

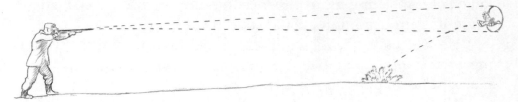

A grouse flying directly ahead of the shooter at eye level should be centered by pointing directly at the bird.

A grouse flying directly ahead of the shooter below eye level should be covered (that is, blotted out) by the muzzle of the gun barrel. Start swing upward; when the bird disappears from view, pull trigger, maintaining upward swing.

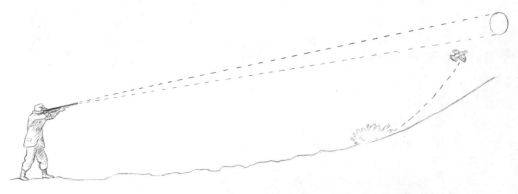

A grouse flying directly ahead of the shooter above eye level and rising sharply should be covered. When bird is blotted out, pull trigger and maintain upward swing.

As we rested on a log, munching on a peanut-butter sandwich, he continued, "You ought to stop for a mite every hundred paces or so. A pa'tridge can't stand sneaky hugger-muggery."

Old Ed and I must have rested in the mellow autumn sunshine for nearly half an hour before starting off again. As we got up, I reached for my gun and snapped the breech shut. At the click, there was a roar of wings behind us. I turned, and my eye caught the flight of a bird disappearing into a cedar thicket before either of us could swing around into position. Amazing how long a grouse will sit tight sometimes.

Looking back, I realize that Old Ed's walk-stop tactic has paid off more than any other bit of wisdom from his storehouse of grouse lore. Now, I come to a complete stop every 20 or 30 yards. Time after time, when I start off again, a grouse will flush at my first step.

Probably the most common shot offered by a grouse is the bird that flushes directly in front of the hunter and flies straight ahead.

As Old Ed and I walked side by side down an old logging road that tunneled through a stand of hardwoods, a bird burst out from the edge, flying straight ahead.

"You take it," Old Ed called out.

Firing twice and missing twice, I shook my head in disbelief. "How could anyone miss such an easy straightaway?"

"Because," Old Ed replied, "that wasn't a straightaway. About the time you shot, he was slantin' down and ducked into the edge of the road again. You should have held under him.

"But when you've got a risin' bird," he continued, "you gotta swing your gun barrel up past him, and when the muzzle covers him, pull that trigger fast! You probably think you've gotta see the bird to hit it. But if you see a risin' bird over your barrel, you're gonna miss him sure."

A few yards farther on, the bird flushed again.

"Your bird," Old Ed called out.

The bird's course was a reasonable facsimile of its first flight. Again it made a dive to the safety of the edge. Confident I knew just where to hold, I swung under the grouse and pressed the trigger.

I turned to Old Ed. "Missed again, didn't I. Now what did I do wrong?"

"Well, the way it looked to me, you was so sure of hittin' him, you raised your head up to watch him drop, just when you touched the trigger."

Again, Old Ed's advice had carry-over value. Although I have occasional lapses, I have pretty well learned to keep my head down and my cheek firmly against the stock.

Descending and rising grouse obviously require a lead below or above the bird. Old Ed would not have had much patience with a technical discussion of vertical or horizontal leads. But instinctively he knew that a bird above eye level flying straight ahead toward that horizon seems, in an optical illusion, to be flying downhill. He didn't need fancy diagrams illustrating this principle of perspective to know he had to hold under the bird to catch up with it—the farther away the bird, the greater the vertical lead needed.

We had come to the end of the logging road, to an area that had been cut over a couple of decades before. On our left was a

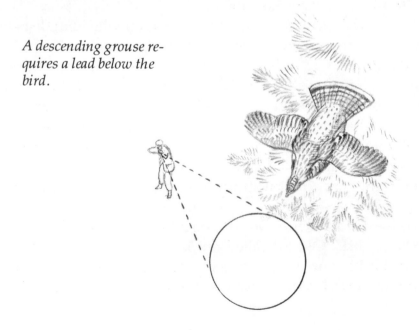

A descending grouse requires a lead below the bird.

It's not easy to remain unflappable and make the right shot when a grouse changes its flight plan.

small plantation of pines, but the remaining terrain had been reseeded by nature.

Fearing Old Ed's patience might be stretched thin, I thought this might be a good time for the pupil to watch the teacher. "You take the next shot," I suggested, "and I'll watch."

We had taken only a few steps when a grouse hurtled out of a small burdock jungle, skimming close to the ground and barreling into the pines. Just as it disappeared, I heard the boom of Old Ed's gun. I assumed he had connected, but a moment later the bird reappeared above the tree line, immediately making a right-angled turn—a rare tactic for a grouse—and started a nosedive back into the pine plantation.

I watched unflappable Old Ed as he shifted his finger to the rear trigger, readjusting instantly to the bird's change of flight plan. At the report, the bird collapsed and dropped straight into the pines.

"How in hell do you ever learn to make a shot like that?" I asked.

"First, you've gotta believe in your gun," he said, giving his

At the report of Old Ed's gun, the grouse dropped.

L. C. Smith 12-gauge double a pat of approval. "After that, it's the learnin' from experience that counts. When you've been shootin' pa'tridge as many years as I have, you'll find out that the critter's got more tricks than a fox tryin' to get in a hen coop. Don't let him fluster you. You've gotta be ready for anythin'."

Old Ed's remarkable shot was the highlight of my initiation into the very specialized art of grouse shooting.

Those were the days I was nibbling at a career in conservation. Shortly after our hunt, Old Ed and I worked together in a field crew on a lake-trout spawn-taking operation at Raquette Lake in the Adirondacks. Our sitting together at the chow table three times a day gave me an opportunity to soak up a lot more of Old Ed's endless store of pointers on grouse shooting.

Although through the years I've tried to practice what Old Ed preached, the more I've tried, the more I am amazed at the countless flush and flight patterns the ruffed grouse presents.

The crossing shot, for example, is another of the many frequently encountered in grouse hunting. The grouse flies in front of the shooter, from right to left or left to right. An interesting shot. Challenging, too, calling for good judgment of distance, flight speed, timing, and angle.

Knowing the angles and where to hold on them is the key to success with a crossing shot. It's difficult to track a bird flying at top speed across your line of vision, usually above eye level. The trick is to keep swinging until the sighting angle is considerably narrowed, holding slightly under, so that the shot charge will be on a collision course with the bird a few feet farther on.

On a crossing shot, I had noticed that Old Ed, instead of just twisting his body, often moved his feet a quarter of a turn in the direction of the bird's flight. Old Ed's maneuver made the shot almost a straightaway.

"The way you shift your feet on that shot is a darned good idea," I told him.

"Do I do that? Must be somethin' I picked up from Pa as a boy."

Old Ed had another maneuver he had picked up from Pa. As every grouse hunter soon learns, the grouse has mastered the trick of quickly putting a tree between itself and the gunner. At the flush, Ed would take a step to one side or the other in a matching bit of cunning that often gave him a clear shot.

I've never been able to master Old Ed's foot-shifting tricks.

On crossing shots (grouse flying perpendicular to your direction of travel), start your swing behind the bird, follow through until there is open space between the bird and your gun's muzzle, pull trigger, and keep following through.

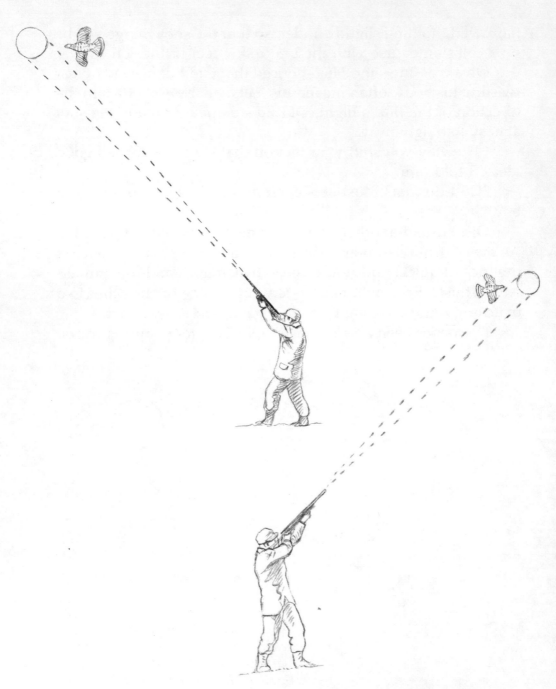

On high crossing shots well above eye level, start swing behind the grouse, holding under and ahead of the bird, and maintain the swing as you pull the trigger.

But because I shoot from the right shoulder, I can usually manage to get a little extra body English at the end of my normal swing on a crossing shot to the left. Sometimes that little extra twist spells the difference between a hit and a miss. But when a bird crosses to my right, I frequently run out of swing before I can line it up.

When I first started grouse hunting, my idea of lead on a crossing shot was a mental picture of punching a hole in the air ahead of the bird and expecting it to fly into the shot charge.

When I told Old Ed about my hole-punching notion, he shook his head.

"It's a wonder you ever hit a pa'tridge," he said. "When a bird crosses in front of you, start your swing behind the bird and keep trackin' it until you get a whisker of daylight in front of the bird just before you shoot. And be sure you keep on swingin' after you pull the trigger."

I have found another advantage in starting the swing behind the bird and following through: it keeps you on the right plane of the bird's line of flight. So even if the bird is rising or descending, you are still on target.

Old Ed's swing-through technique on crossing birds has improved my score more than any gunning tip of the many he gave me. But in the hilly coverts I hunt around my home today, I'm continually challenged by uphill and downhill shots that I never encountered in Old Ed's flat Oneida Lake country. If not climbing a hogback, I'm dipping down a gully.

My most troublesome shot takes place on what I call summit meetings with the ruffed grouse. A bird is flying uphill and should be covered, but just as I have it blotted from view and pull the trigger, that grouse suddenly becomes a descending target as it drops to safety on the other side of the hill. Although I desperately try to reverse my lead to under the bird for a second shot, my timing and reflexes are seldom equal to the test.

Every once in a while a grouse flies straight toward me, just above eye level. Skeet shooters know this shot as the incomer at No. 8 station. "Start your swing under the bird," they tell me, "and come up past the bird. When it is blotted out, pull the trigger."

Some accomplished grouse hunters, I've noticed, do not attempt the shot as an incomer. Instead, they calmly turn around and take the bird as an ordinary going-away shot.

How easy it is to diagram typical grouse shots, but how difficult it is to make them in the field. Diagrams pinpoint a grouse's presumed flight pattern. But in the wild, a grouse sets its own unpredictable course, and circumstances—predicaments is a better word—vary from the ground you are standing on to the geometry of your shooting stance. Seldom are both feet solidly placed. Most of the time you're off balance when the bird goes up. Perhaps you're stepping over a log or slipping down a steep hillside. You may have to part tree branches with your gun barrel to get a shot, or shield your face when you push through a tangle of briers.

Nor does a diagram take into account a myriad of other conditions. Sometimes it's the weather, for better or worse. A day following a night of rain seems to produce the best hunting, the wet ground making everything quiet underfoot. Strong winds seem to produce the worst hunting—often you can't hear a bird going up, and grouse become jittery, flushing out of range. A case can even be made for the influence of solunar phenomena on hunting success. Even for barometric pressure: with a low glass, *Bonasa* seems to lie low. Or light intensity: on cloudy days, birds often present a blurred image over a gun barrel; on bright days, the silhouette is clear and sharp.

Besides an endless variety of field conditions that influence the actual shooting part of ruffed-grouse hunting, you are up against a gamebird with a diabolical diversity of maneuvers.

As gun editor Capt. Paul Curtis[14] noted, "To be a successful grouse hunter one must be more than a good shot, he must be a student of the game he pursues."

Old Ed was not a student, but he was a natural naturalist. His version was: "If you want to shoot 'em, you've got to know where to find 'em. Don't just look for birds, look for signs, too:

tracks, feathers, roostin's, dustin's, droppin's, scratchin's. And always keep listenin'—sometimes the cluck of a pa'tridge will give away its hidin' place."

Over second helpings at the chow table during our perpetual pa'tridge talk, he included bits of his woodland wisdom.

"On quiet days, when there's no wind blowin'," he said, "look for a swirl of leaves up ahead. Probably means a pa'tridge has just taken off without makin' a noise."

Another tip has become a part of my hunting routine: "Never pass up a brush pile without givin' it a boot. Most times if somethin' comes out, it'll be a cottontail. But every once in a while it'll be a pa'tridge."

Several of my backyard coverts are studded with ground junipers—good escape cover for grouse—and the brush-pile ploy produces a bird often enough to make it worthwhile to detour here and there to give every juniper bush a hefty kick.

When Old Ed was looking for grouse, his on-the-job training gave him a practical knowledge of nature's interrelationships that was as good in some ways as an ecology course in college.

But this is not to downgrade the scientific approach. Indeed, looking back, I now realize that next to Old Ed's walk-stop tactic, my most productive bit of hunting strategy came from the academic world. It grew from a discussion of Aldo Leopold's "edge theory" in Frank Edminster's class in Game Management at Cornell.

In the anatomy of ruffed-grouse hunting, edge is the connective tissue that holds a good covert together. Leopold was one of the first to point out the significance of these wildlife borders, noting that game is actually a phenomenon of edges and game occurs where the right combination of food and cover come together.

Leopold had the knack of describing the concept in words all hunters understand: ". . . the quail hunter follows the common *edge* between the bushy draw and the weedy corn, the snipe hunter the *edge* between the marsh and the pasture, the deer hunter the *edge* between the oaks of the south slope and the pine thickets of the north slope, the rabbit hunter the grassy *edge* of the thicket. Even the duck hunter sets his stool on the *edge* between the tules and the celery beds. . . ."

And zeroing in on *Bonasa,* Leopold states: "Every grouse hunter knows this when he selects the *edge* of a woods, with its grape tangles, haw-bushes and little grassy bays, as the likely place to look for birds."

The best spots to look for grouse are where a grouse's favorite types of cover converge to form distinct edges. But any kind of edge is better than no edge. That's why woods, roads, trails, and fire lanes are generally productive.

But even when a gunner works these productive edges, some shots will be missed and some birds will go up out of range. So it's helpful to know what type of cover a grouse will fly to if it has a choice.

On short hops, the bird naturally settles down in the same type of cover it took off from. On longer flights, a grouse also has a strong bent to set down in the same type of cover from which it originally flushed.

An exception is that grouse flushed from open lands such as pastures—a rare occurrence—prefer to fly to thicker cover, regardless of the flight's distance.

Evergreens (either pure stands of conifers or conifers mixed with hardwoods) are also a favorite escape cover for a flushed grouse.

Here again, I've learned the ruffed grouse comes off as an individualist. One season, an abandoned hilltop apple orchard held two birds. I flushed them on nearly every visit but could never get a good, clear shot.

One bird, whose territory was near the edge of the orchard, invariably headed for nearby hardwoods. The other bird, whose bailiwick was just as close to the hardwoods, always made a longer flight over a ravine to a pine thicket.

By devising a plan built around the two birds' flush patterns, I managed to crop both birds before the season ended.

It is through just such experiences in the field that a grouse gunner gains knowledge of a grouse's habits—snippets of grouse lore that will pay off throughout his hunting life. As John Locke long ago said: "No man's knowledge can go beyond his experience."

A grouse gunner also learns from experience that he has at least one advantage on his side: a ruffed grouse will usually permit a hunter to get fairly close before flushing. In fact, sometimes too close—roaring up from under your feet. The close, centered shot that follows renders the bird unfit for the pot—or, "fricasseed," as Old Ed called it.

Most grouse will flush within 50 feet of the hunter. That finding is confirmed by the New York State Ruffed Grouse Investigation. A study—the only one of its kind—of 16,688 flushes showed that 12,742 birds flushed within 50 feet of the observer. Even so, it wouldn't surprise me if the clever grouse sensed that the field crew weren't carrying guns.

A breakdown of the data shows that if a grouse is flushed in the clear, usually there's no need to push the panic button. The bird generally is close enough for you to have plenty of time to line it up before it gets out of range.

No. of Grouse	Distance from Observer When Flushed
1,947	0– 10 feet
3,397	11–20 feet
3,284	21–30 feet
1,996	31–40 feet
2,118	41–50 feet
728	51–60 feet
346	61–70 feet
923	71–80 feet
91	81–90 feet
1,175	91– 100 feet
683	Over 100 feet
16,688	

No. of Grouse	Distance from Flush to Reflush
59	0–50 feet
146	51–100 feet
202	101–150 feet
261	151–200 feet
110	201–250 feet
325	251–300 feet
58	301–350 feet
115	351–400 feet
43	401–450 feet
55	451–500 feet
90	Over 500 feet
1,464	

Another aid to the grouse gunner to come out of the Investigation were measurements of how far the grouse flew from the point of the original flush to where the bird was reflushed.

Information on 1464 flushes gives a gunner an idea of what to expect. Although a grouse allowed the observer to approach fairly close before flushing, once airborne, it seemed hellbent on getting off and away. Almost half of the birds that flushed flew from 250 to over 500 feet before setting down again.

Most ruffed grouse are likely to flush from the ground. That characteristic, observed by most hunters, was confirmed by the New York State Ruffed Grouse Investigation: of 16,253 flushes, 13,191 originated from the ground, 3062 from a tree.

One surprise: though the majority of grouse flushed from the ground on the original flush, nearly two-thirds chose a tree in which to alight. Of the 1352 reflushes, 841 were from a tree and 511 from the ground.

This finding doesn't seem to jibe with my own experience. Even late in the season, when I find birds favoring conifers or "budding" in the hardwoods and the original flush is from a tree, most of the grouse I reflush take off from the ground.

Of course, some birds in conifers may be giving me the slip. Hidden in a hemlock, *Bonasa* may be looking down at me with its penetrating eye, supremely confident, while I shuffle around checking every likely bit of ground cover.

A flushed grouse, marked down, always rekindles my enthusiasm. Now that I have a definite bird to work on, the anticipation of getting a shot pumps adrenaline into my system, giving me new energy for the search.

Through the years, I've worked out a tactic that has greatly improved my odds in reflushing a bird. When a grouse touches down, it usually walks or runs a few steps, continuing in the same direction before freezing. My early shooting companions taught me to go directly to the bird's point of landing and then search around that point in ever-widening circles.

As I put this technique into practice, it seemed to me that this "inside-out" kind of attack encouraged the bird to keep on moving and then take to the air again, out of range.

So I hit upon an "outside-in" system. When I miss a shot, or the bird goes up out of range, I'm in luck in marking it down if I catch the direction the bird veers as it sideslips at the end of its flight—a typical trait of the grouse. I make a wide swing around the spot I think the bird is, and then I infiltrate its territory in narrowing concentric circles—working from the outside in, instead of from the inside out.

This is no time, however, for Old Ed's walk-stop operation. I keep walking at a steady pace, which often makes the bird freeze. The outside-in circling tactic seems to make the bird uncertain of what is going on around it. When the closing-in suspense becomes unbearable, the grouse takes off, often within easy range.

Sometimes a real smart grouse puts on a counteroffensive by keeping on the move and outflanking me. Suddenly there is a roar of wings and in the periphery of my vision I catch a subliminal image of the bird flying out of range, snooting me with avian arrogance.

But trying to outmaneuver *Bonasa* is the story of any grouse

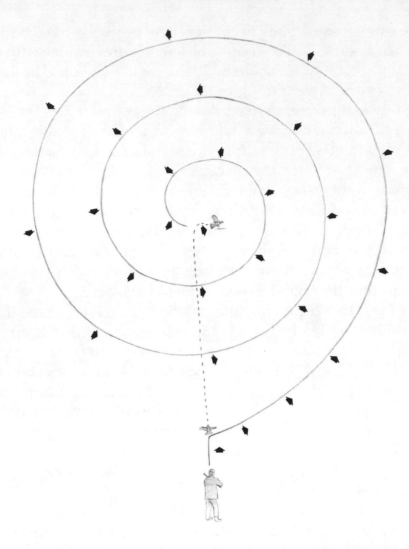

Here's the Heacox ''outside-in'' system of searching for a grouse that's been marked down.

hunter's gunning life. Successful grouse gunning is really structured hunting. Mapping out a kind of mental blueprint before starting a hunt may not always add weight to the game bag, but it always adds interest to the hunting experience. Such structured strategy also pays a compliment to the quality of the quarry.

An accomplished grouse gunner's roving eye is constantly interpreting cover types, searching for edge situations, and ferreting out the bird's options of escape routes. The hunter is always anticipating a flush, yet always surprised when the flush does come. Then, in an instant, the scene becomes a problem of space, time, and motion: the relationship of space to the flying speed of the grouse and the effect of angle and perspective.

This is the moment that everything the grouse hunter has ever learned and all the wiles bred into countless generations of ruffed grouse come together. It's the moment for the most important element of all—concentration, an essential of successful shooting often overlooked.

The importance of concentration was impressed on me in our backyard hunting trips by my neighbor and fellow grouse hunter, the late Frederic "Pete" Bontecou, who was tutored in wingshooting by Oakleigh Thorne, one of the world's best trap and field shots in the early part of the century. Thorne's credentials included winning the London Gun Club International Cup and the Grand Prix de Paris in the same year.

"To be a good wingshooter," Pete always maintained, "takes intense concentration from the moment of flush until you pull the trigger. It shouldn't be that reflex action a grouse so often traps us into. A cool and controlled shooter is a consistent shooter."

Bernard Baruch, park-bench philosopher and advisor to Presidents, might have been speaking of grouse gunners with his formula: "Success observes the future and acts before it happens."

I have observed that the best grouse gunners invariably are endowed with this special gift: the ability to anticipate the problem and, at flash point, the ability to come up with the solution.

But *Bonasa* is also endowed with a talent for coming up with a solution at flash point. And that is what adds the incomparable zest to ruffed-grouse hunting.

11

One-to-One
Grouse Hunting

That matchless zest, for me, reaches its zenith on those glowing autumn days when I am alone in a grouse covert and waiting for the first stirring wingbeat, signaling *Bonasa* has entered the scene.

A special chemistry between two natural loners establishes a rapport, turning the meeting from just a high-velocity encounter into a fulfilling woodland experience—a private affair between the grouse and me.

Not that I don't look back on many great grouse hunts with good companions. But after enjoying solo, duet, and group hunting over the years, I have come to the realization that one-to-one hunting, for me, is closest to the true essence of grouse hunting. To lean back against a tree and watch a red-tailed hawk soaring majestically on the Harlem Valley thermals; to feast my eyes on the crimson jewels of partridgeberry; to be accepted by a chickadee or a chipmunk as part of the landscape as I rest on a stonewall; or to be amazed anew each year by witch hazel, whose fringelike yellow blossoms turn autumn into spring—like the ruffed grouse, itself, bringing life to a fading fall scene.

If it were not for the quiet interludes of solo grouse hunting, I probably would never have had the thrill of seeing my first and only pileated woodpecker. Still sharply etched in memory are its sweeping wingbeats, flashing black-and-white markings, and brilliant red crest.

In the give-and-take interplay of one-to-one hunting, the quest becomes an intriguing game. I pit my years of experience, sharpened by Old Ed's stratagems and augmented by an academic knowledge of cover, against a fast-flying grouse whose endless deceptions add suspense to the outcome of each confrontation.

Even the company of a good bird dog can intrude on that special relationship between hunter and bird in one-to-one grouse hunting. But to inquire whether to hunt with or without a dog is a loaded question. It's a sure way to get into a crossfire of hot debate.

There's no doubt that a good dog will add to the number of cripples recovered. From my point of view, that's the greatest advantage of hunting grouse with a dog.

I think back to a grouse hunt with Albert Hall, an alumnus of the New York State Grouse Investigation who went on to become Director of the New York State Division of Fish and Game. We were having a fine day in one of Al's favorite coverts near his Catskill home, accompanied by Chief, a powerfully built black Labrador.

A big brown-phase grouse went up on my side, its reddish-brown tail catching the sun as it gained altitude. I fired twice, the shots echoing down through the Delaware Valley.

No puff of feathers. No quiver. No indication I had hit the bird.

I spent several minutes explaining to Al what made me miss. Just as I was running out of alibis, the Lab came out of the woods, a big bird in its mouth—a big bird with a distinctive rufous tail.

And I've had some outstanding grouse-hunting days when an exceptional dog took charge. There was that Adirondack hunt near Lake of the Woods with Victor Coty. A day when his English setter, Queen, at the peak of her perfection and working close and frequently checking our whereabouts, enabled us to shoot our limit, both of us for the first time, in one of the most effortless grouse hunts I can remember.

But dogs have also had a role in some of my worst hunts. I recall a disastrous day when a so-called grouse dog, in a wild, four-hour romp, flushed every bird far ahead of our guns, often completely out of sight.

It must have been just such an infuriating experience that led Colonel Harold P. Sheldon,[39] a Vermont-based grouse hunter and authoritative outdoor writer, to issue a manifesto about hunting grouse with a dog: "Rather than undergo the exasperation of endeavoring to use a second-rate dog for this game, the writer, for one, infinitely prefers to shoot with no dog at all. . . . An experienced shot who knows how to beat his ground can bag as many birds without a dog as with one."

In open-cover hunting—for pheasant and quail, for instance—there's no question but that the dog's role is one of the sweetest sights for a hunter's eyes: a big, strong pointer ranging a field in great sweeps; then a careful quartering, covering every bit of ground with no lost motion; and suddenly, on point, turning into a sculpture. The whole act performed onstage in full view of the gunner.

But when the ruffed grouse is the quarry, so much of the action takes place offstage that the pleasure of viewing the performance is lost. If the dog is working in thick cover, which is par for the course with grouse, it is frequently out of sight of the gunner for long periods. Indeed, a hunter may spend most of his time trying to find his dog, which he senses is on point somewhere in the vicinity. And the ruffed grouse, itself, doesn't take kindly to a pushy dog and will invariably flush wild.

Although hunting with a dog may sometimes add weight to the game bag, it can also subtract from the unique quality of the grouse-hunting experience. So there are a lot of us out there in the coverts who subscribe to the credo: to savor grouse hunting at its best is to hunt a covert as a solitary hunter.

And because I hunt the same coverts, season after season, I encounter the more elusive grouse time after time, which turns the hunt into a perennial private transaction.

For a few years, I kept a running account of these transactions with *Bonasa*. There is probably not a member of the grouse-gunning guild, novice or master, who has not wondered how many shells it takes to bag one grouse. Or the miles he walks to bag a grouse or just to flush a grouse. Or how many hours he spends seeking, searching, stalking—and sometimes even shagging—the strong-willed bird.

To check on my own hunting, I acquired a pedometer and stuffed a notebook and stub pencil into a shell pocket. I suspect any schoolboy of today, with his pocket calculator, would scoff at my system.

In tallying the score sheets, I found the grouse was the winner by a large margin. In these dealings, the grouse always gave full value as a gamebird, never less than its best. Difficult to find, hard to hit, and after lift-off, always flying at top speed.

For grouse hunters who want to compare records, here's what some amateurish extrapolation of four years of scorekeeping turned up in hunting my backyard coverts. These coverts are interesting to work, but their forest succession has passed the most productive stage for grouse habitat. Furthermore, the area is undergoing the usual encroachments of an area 75 miles from New York City.

During my recordkeeping years, I hunted from 23 to 30 days

a season. A grouse season, for me, is usually from opening day until the first snowfall or the time the deer-hunting season opens, when our quiet coverts tend to become overcrowded.

Since I seldom hunt all day, the number of hours I spend in the coverts is a better basis for determining the amount of time I devote to the sport. A span of time, the record shows, ranging from 48 to 88 hours a season (averaging out to 63 hours) for the 4-year period and from 2 to 3 hours a day. It didn't surprise me to learn that it took me between 15 and 16 hours of hunting time to bag one grouse.

What did surprise me, though, was the number of miles I traveled a season. It varied from 120 miles to 220 miles, totaling 623 miles for the period, and averaging out to 38 miles of walking to put one grouse in the bag.

I like to burn powder and pull the trigger whenever there's a reasonable chance of scoring a hit, my conscience guiding my judgment along that thin line separating what should be a solid hit from a shot that might merely wound a bird.

Although the number of grouse I flushed varied from 34 in the poorest year to 68 in the best, I accepted only 15 shots during a season in which birds were scarce and up to 26 shots in a season they were more plentiful. The number of birds harvested varied from 2 to 6 a season and required from 4 to 5 shots each.

It was heartening to find that I made most of my successful shots on the first barrel. When I missed with the first barrel, however, I frequently missed with the second barrel, too. I seem constitutionally incapable of putting into practice the tip Lou Smith gave me years ago about single-trigger doubles: when you miss with the first barrel, drop the gun from the shoulder, then remount with the hope of correcting the alignment.

The scorekeeping years coincided with years grouse were in short supply. My image as a shooter might have been enhanced if some bonanza years had been included.

The year 1967 helped my image. Not that birds were so plentiful; it was just that I never shot better. But the very next year I slipped into a horrendous slump, the kind that bruises a hunter's ego and warps his personality.

After I finished tallying the grouse-hunting seasons, I was impressed once more with the compelling magnetism of this incomparable bird. It's an attraction that keeps drawing me—and a faithful following of several million other grouse hunters—back to the coverts season after season.

The powerful pull takes me back in fat years—and in lean ones like 1968, when I worked the coverts 88 hours and walked 220 miles to bag 2 grouse.

The amazing amount of time expended, the astonishing number of miles traveled, and the strong individuality of the ruffed grouse are dramatized by my encounter with "the grouse that roared."

I'm free to hunt nearly every day during the season, and I have a choice of a dozen different backyard coverts. So in my one-to-one style of hunting, I get to know certain grouse as individuals with distinctive personalities.

The grouse most sharply etched in my memory was a big, gray bird. This ebullient creature, overflowing with high spirits, had a takeoff that was marked by an unusually loud decibel count, ending in a Wagnerian crescendo.

Frank Booth, a farmer neighbor, and part of my intelligence network, first told me about this bird one day when I met him on a tractor in his woodlot.

"I see one of your 'crazy birds' most every morning. Struttin' along where the two paths meet west of the old hay barn. He's a big gray one, and he sure makes a heck of a racket when he goes up."

Except on opening day, when it's a sacrilege not to be afield soon after sun-up, my inherited New England Puritan work ethic keeps me at my desk in the morning. So my attempt to locate the bird in its afternoon territory turned out to be a real chore. A week of postmeridian scouting, though, finally paid off.

I had been working along the edges of the trails where Frank had spotted the bird, when I heard an explosive thundering of wings in the woods about 30 yards away.

"That's got to be Frank's bird," my ears told me, as I raised my gun. But the resounding roar of the flush broke my concen-

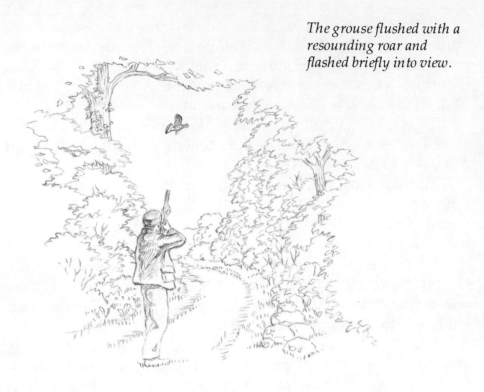

The grouse flushed with a resounding roar and flashed briefly into view.

tration. As the bird came into view, I—like a dub beginner—fired two wild shots in its general direction.

I marked down the bird as it set its wings for a landing. But this time, my outside-in circling tactic did not work.

I explored the covert for future reference. A lightly wooded piece of about a hundred acres, shaped like an Indian arrowhead. In its center was a little cul-de-sac carpeted with a luxuriant growth of partridgeberry, flanked on one side with white birches. On the other side stood young maples dominated by two big-boled beech trees. Adjoining this patch was a small stand of white pines that Frank had planted ten years before. A hedgerow along the edge of a town dirt road was lined with viburnums loaded with berries. Across the road was an abandoned orchard, its limbs hanging heavy with apples. In other words, a perfect grousescape.

Just as I like to locate a big trout and try to outwit it, I get an extra charge when I have a special bird to work on. For the rest of the season, I checked the covert regularly. The bird, seemingly calculating his margin of safety to the nearest tantalizing foot, would invariably go up just at the edge of my Ithaca's range.

The next year, I continued to monitor the covert industriously about once a week, meeting the big gray bird often enough to keep the feud interesting.

It was pretty much a rerun of the first year. The grouse continued its frustrating pattern of going up out of range, every flush accenting the bird's characteristic exuberance. And my shooting also kept to the original script of missing with both barrels. Occasionally, in heavy cover, the edge of the shot pattern would riddle a few leaves. But as far as I could tell, I didn't even tickle the tail of the bird.

In a countering tactic, I lugged "Elsie" around for a few hunts, hoping that the 12-gauge would connect on one of those long shots. The shift didn't pay off. I was glad to switch back to the lighter Ithaca.

Now and then I sweetened up the shooting with a bird from another covert. But the challenge of the big gray bird kept drawing me back. That second season came to a close, and my only reward was the mighty roar of the big gray bird's flush.

The third year, I didn't flush the bird on my first trip out. Or the second. Or the third. Since the average life-span of the ruffed grouse, in the wild, is less than three years, I began to suspect the bird had surrendered to the inevitable.

The second year of chasing the big gray bird was a rerun of frustration.

Our first rendezvous of that season did not come until late October, the flush marked by a sonic intensity that could only be the big gray grouse. That year, the bird selected the partridge-berry patch as its favorite spot.

The old warrior, now a patriarch of the coverts, was full of geriatric jauntiness. The bird's *pro-forma* escape tactic was at its peak, and my shooting performance was grooved in its familiar sad syndrome.

Near the end of the season, a new stratagem flashed through my mind. Always starting the hunt from the junction of the two trails at the edge of Frank's woodlot, I had become just as much a creature of habit as the grouse. "Perhaps," I thought, "if I circle around and come in by the back door, the bird will be puzzled and sit tight long enough to let me get within range before flushing."

It was a cold day, with the smell of snow in the air when I started out. To make sure I didn't telegraph my new game plan, I circled around some 50 yards out from the center of the covert before heading for the focal point of the bird's domain—the par-tridgeberry patch.

As I looked ahead, a glimpse of bright-red berries signaled I was nearing the spot. I tensed up, primed for action. Moving slowly ahead, expecting the expected, I felt my heart thump. It sounded, to my ears, not unlike the drumming of a distant grouse. I took a deep breath, trying to steady myself for the flush. But there was no flush.

"I should have known," I thought, "that old bird is too smart to fall for my back-door approach."

Admitting I'd met my match, I headed for home. At my first step, there was a great roar of wings behind me. I swung around to see the huge gray bird coming toward me a few feet overhead, much too close to shoot.

Again I turned around sharply, throwing myself off balance. The grouse veered off to the left—my better shooting side—at a slight angle, in the clear, but rapidly getting out of range.

I swung up from behind on my target, trying desperately, as

A wide circle was an attempt to disguise the new plan.

The big gray grouse came straight ahead, much too close for a shot.

Then the grouse veered off to the left at a slight angle, in the clear.

I lined it up over the gun barrel, to get that precious "whisker of daylight" ahead of the bird. But I didn't quite get it. However, the fringe of the shot pattern momentarily altered the bird's suspension. For a split-second, the grouse yawed a little to the right, then moved ahead again at full speed. But that split second of hesitation gave me a chance to realign my shot.

At the report, the bird's wings folded. I watched the big gray grouse drop with a soft thud. I hurried to the spot. There lay the majestic creature on a bed of russet leaves, wings beating a final, muffled tattoo.

As I stood there in the fading light of a late-November day, those bittersweet feelings welled up as they did when I shot my first grouse at Cascade Ridge. Doggedness and a lucky tactic had achieved what, for me, was a minor miracle.

A few snowflakes drifted down as I picked up the bird, its gray mantle a toga of distinction. The finality of it all suddenly struck home. The three-year chase was over, the quest finished, the goal gained.

Now, instead of a feeling of triumph, I was aware only of an overwhelming sense of loss. Something very special had gone out of my life—the mighty "grouse that roared." A gallant gamebird whose vital spirit had transformed each one-to-one encounter into a never-to-be-forgotten grouse-hunting adventure.

12
Parting Shot

The ruffed grouse is a lusty testimonial to a gamebird at its best. A native, continental treasure—the touchstone by which all other North American gamebirds are measured.

To those wingshooters who value dash and style in their upland-bird hunting, the ruffed grouse, handsome and high-spirited, is a gallant quarry. Admired, prized, respected.

In no other kind of wingshooting is the hunt dominated by such interplay between the gunner and his quarry. A special relationship, leaving the hunter with remembrances of hunts past glowing in memory.

For legions of grouse hunters, the charisma of the bird and the ambiance of its environment create a mystique that turns ruffed-grouse hunting into a magnificent obsession.

Gunning for grouse is an enduring blend of yesterday and today, upholding the best traditions of American hunting. Aldo Leopold,[29] the most discerning interpreter of our ruffed-grouse heritage, wrote: "There are two kinds of hunting, ordinary hunting and ruffed-grouse hunting."

Ordinary hunting is something you do. Ruffed-grouse hunting is something you are.

This gallant gamebird's vital spirit has led the author to unforgettable adventure.

Acknowledgments

As always, I am grateful to Dottie, my wife and writing partner. Working side by side with me, she comes up, time after time, with a better word to express a thought, a smoother transition or a clearer expression of a technical sequence. And, finally, as an accomplished secretary, she edits and types with nimble fingers the finished product.

In compiling the story of *Bonasa umbellus*, I traveled by letter to every part of the bird's vast North American range.

As a former member of the New York State Conservation Department, I found it heartening that the double-barreled spirit of cooperation and conservation still stands. Replies to my queries came winging back from every state, province, and territory I contacted. Indeed, many quotations were taken from their letters because they were, by far, better than any words the author could write.

In my letters, I purposely avoided revealing my strong emotional involvement with the grouse. I soon made the discovery that others shared my feelings for the gallant grouse.

In this vein, Mark Dilts put it this way:

"When I became editor-publisher of *The Drummer*, official publication of The Ruffed Grouse Society, I assumed, for some unknown reason, that I was one of the relatively few people who held the ruffed grouse in such awe and respect. I learned very quickly, however, that I had misjudged the entire grouse-hunting fraternity.

"Being in constant contact with grouse hunters throughout much of the country, as I am, I find similar feelings for this fabled bird of the puckerbrush to be a part of every serious grouse hunter I have ever met."

Particular recognition goes to Gardiner Bump, Robert W. Darrow, Walter F. Crissey, and the late Frank C. Edminster for the valued use made of their book, *The Ruffed Grouse: Life History — Propagation — Management*, a magisterial volume of 951 pages based on the work of the New York State Grouse Investigation.

I am indebted to John W. Aldrich, Research Associate, National Museum of Natural History, Smithsonian Institution, for permission to use material from his writings on the taxonomic classification of *Bonasa umbellus* and subspecies, and the bird's environmental orientations.

Also to Gordon W. Gullion, Associate Professor and Leader, Forest Wildlife Project, University of Minnesota, for permission to quote from his published works. His forthcoming book based on 22 years of research is awaited by both professional conservationists and grouse hunters.

And to Dr. David P. Olson, Director, Institute of Natural and Environmental Resources, for information on prescribed burning as a tool of game management.

I am grateful to Leo Martin, of the former Abercrombie & Fitch Company, New York, for sharing his storehouse of knowledge about guns and grouse gunning gear. And to Richard Baldwin, Remington Arms Company, for guidance in diagramming the shooting sketches.

Appreciated also is the help of Helen Rogers in translating material written in French from the Province of Quebec; and the help of

Lois Rigoulot, Librarian of the Millbrook Free Library, and her staff for assistance in getting valuable reference material.

Special thanks go to Carl Parker, Chief, Bureau of Fish, New York State Department of Environmental Conservation, a truly dedicated grouse hunter and superb shot for making available his extensive collection of grouse tails to the book's illustrator, Wayne Trimm.

For current information on the bird, itself, its range, hunting harvests, research, management and sidelights on the ruffed-grouse story, I am indebted to dozens of conservation workers in the states, provinces, and territories for their contributions.

In the United States:

Ralph H. Allen, Jr., Chief, Game Management Section, Alabama Department of Conservation and Natural Resources; Jerry D. McGowan, Game Biologist, Alaska Department of Fish and Game; Mitchell J. Rogers, Forest Game Biologist, Arkansas Game and Fish Commission; Harold T. Harper, Upland Game Coordinator, California Department of Fish and Game; Harvey S. Donoho, Small Game Program Supervisor, Colorado Division of Wildlife; George E. Brys, Wildlife Research Biologist, Connecticut Department of Environmental Protection; Thomas W. Whittendale, Jr., Wildlife Biologist, Delaware Division of Fish and Wildlife; Joe Kurz, Assistant Chief, Game Management Section, Georgia Department of Natural Resources; Dick Norell, State Game Bird Supervisor, Idaho Department of Fish and Game; John C. Calhoun, Chief, Forest Game Section, and Forrest D. Loomis, Forest Game Biologist, Illinois Department of Conservation; P. Decker Major, Biologist, Indiana Department of Natural Resources; Terry W. Little, Forest Research Biologist, Iowa Conservation Commission; James S. Durrell, Assistant Director, Division of Game Management, Kentucky Department of Fish and Wildlife Resources; Lee E. Perry, Assistant Chief, Wildlife Division, and Frederick B. Hurley, Jr., Wildlife Resource Planner, Maine Department of Fisheries and Wildlife; Eugene F. Deems, Jr., Conservation Information, Maryland Department of Natural Resources; Michael Pollack, Chief Game Biologist, and Richard E. Burrell, Assistant Game Biologist, Massachusetts Division of Fisheries and Game; Herbert E. Johnson, Northern Game Bird Management, and Lawrence D. Fay, D.V.M., In Charge, Pathology and Physiology Research, Michigan Department of Natural Resources; Roger Holmes, Chief, Section of Wildlife, Minnesota Department of Natural Resources; Kenneth M. Babcock, Assistant Chief, Wildlife Division, and John Lewis, Wildlife Research Biologist, Missouri Department of Conservation; Dr. John P. Weigand, Fish and Wildlife Biology

Supervisor, Montana Department of Fish and Game; Glen C. Christensen, Chief of Game Division, Nevada Department of Fish and Game; Hilbert R. Siegler, Chief of Game Management and Research and Donald G. Allison, Wildlife Biologist, New Hampshire Fish and Game Department; Robert C. Lund, Principal Wildlife Biologist, New Jersey Department of Environmental Protection; Herbert Doig, Assistant Commissioner for Natural Resources, New York State Department of Environmental Conservation; Charles E. Hill, Supervising Wildlife Biologist, North Carolina Wildlife Resources Commission; John W. Schulz, Upland Game Management Biologist, and Larry Kruckenberg, Information Specialist, North Dakota Game and Fish Department; Robert J. Stoll, Wildlife Biologist, Ohio Department of Natural Resources; Chester E. Kebbe, Staff Biologist, Oregon Department of Fish and Wildlife; Dale E. Sheffer, Chief, Division of Game Management, Pennsylvania Game Commission; John M. Cronan, Chief, Rhode Island Division of Fish and Wildlife; Sam W. Stokes, District Biologist, South Carolina Wildlife and Marine Resources Department; Theron E. Schenck, Assistant Regional Supervisor, Game Management, and Ron Fowler, Game Staff Specialist, South Dakota Division of Game and Fish; John C. Kruzan, Chief of Wildlife Management and Clifton J. Whitehead, Jr., Wildlife Research Supervisor, Tennessee Wildlife Resources Agency; Norman V. Hancock, Chief, Game Management, Utah Division of Wildlife Resources; Ben Day, Chief Wildlife Biologist, and Robert Candy, Chief, Information and Education, Vermont Department of Fish and Game; Joe L. Coggin, Supervising Game Biologist, Virginia Commission of Game and Inland Fisheries; C. Fred Martinsen, Supervisor, Small Game Management, Washington Department of Game; James W. Rawson, Assistant Supervisor, Wildlife Planning, West Virginia Department of Natural Resources; John M. Keener, Director, Bureau of Wildlife Management, Wisconsin Department of Natural Resources; and Rex M. Corsi, State Game Warden, Wyoming Game and Fish Department.

In the Dominion of Canada:

Blair Rippin, Regional Wildlife Biologist, Alberta Division of Fish and Wildlife; G. A. Ferguson and R. J. Stevens, Public Information Officers, British Columbia Department of Recreation and Conservation; R. B. Oetting, Wildlife Biologist, Manitoba Department of Renewable Resources and Transportation Services; J. C. Baird, Wildlife Biologist, New Brunswick Department of Natural Resources; Michael Strapp, Statistician, Wildlife Division, Newfoundland Department of Tourism; Neil van Nostrand, Upland Game Biologist, Nova Scotia Department of Lands and Forests; Richard L. Séguin, Director, Wildlife Management Service, and Clément Veilleux, Director, Wildlife Management and Exploitation Branch, Québec Direction Generale de la Faune; J. Douglas Roseborough, Director, Wildlife Branch, Ontario Ministry of Natural Resources; Alan P. Godfrey, Upland Game Biologist, Fish and Wildlife Division, Prince Edward Island Department of the Environment; David S. Gray, Provincial Bird Ecologist, and D. Mevel, Resource Officer, Fisheries and Wildlife Branch, Saskatchewan Department of Tourism and Renewable Resources; Winnie Kaptein, Fish and Wildlife Service, Northwest Territories Department of Natural and Cultural Affairs; and Dave Mossop, Ornithologist, Game Branch, Government of the Yukon Territory.

Bibliography

Text References

Numbers at the left edge correspond to the superior figures placed at appropriate spots throughout the text. —Editor's note.

1. Aldrich, John W.: "Geographic Orientation of American Tetraonidae" *Journal of Wildlife Management,* October 1963.
2. Allen, Arthur A. See Bent, A. C.
3. ——:"Sights and Sounds of the Winged World," *National Geographic Magazine,* June 1945.

4. Anonymous. *The American Shooters Manual by a Gentleman of Philadelphia*, Carey, Lea and Carey, Philadelphia, 1827.
5. ———: *The Sportsman's Companion or an Essay on Shooting*, New York, 1783. Reprinted by Stackpole and Heck, Harrisburg, Pa., 1948.
6. Audubon, John J.: *The Birds of America*, V. G. Audubon, New York, 1856.
7. Bartram, John: See Edwards, G.
8. Bent, Arthur C.: *Life Histories of North American Gallinaceous Birds*, U.S. National Museum, Smithsonian Bulletin 162, 1932.
9. Brewster, William.: "The Ruffed Grouse Again," *American Sportsman*, 4 (1), 1874.
10. Bump, Gardiner, Robert W. Darrow, Frank C. Edminster, and Walter F. Crissey. *The Ruffed Grouse*, New York State Conservation Department, Albany, 1947. Reprinted by The Loyal Order of Dedicated Grouse Hunters, Cleveland, 1978.
11. Connett, Eugene V. ed.: *Upland Game Bird Shooting In America*, Derrydale Press, New York, 1930.
12. Crissey, Walter F.: See Bump, G.
13. Curtis, Paul A.: *Guns and Gunning*, Penn Publishing Co., Philadelphia, 1934.
14. ———: *American Game Shooting*, E. P. Dutton, 1927.
15. Darrow, Robert W.: See Bump, G.
16. Denys, Nicholas: *Description and Natural History of the Coasts of North America*, Champlain Society Publications 2, 1908.
17. Douglas, David: "Observations on Some Species of the Genera Tetrao and Ortyx, Natives of North America," *Transactions of Linnaean Society of London*, 16 (1), 1833.
18. Edminster, Frank C.: See Bump, G.
19. ———: *The Ruffed Grouse*, Macmillan, New York, 1947.
20. Edwards, George W.: "On the Pheasant of Pennsylvania, the Otis Minor," *Philosophical Transactions, Royal Society of London*, 10 (63), 1754.
21. Elliott, Daniel: *The Gallinaceous Game Birds of North America*, Suckling & Co, London, 1897.
22. Etchen, Fred: *Common Sense Shotgun Shooting*, Standard Publications, Huntington, West Virginia, 1946.
23. Fay, L. Dale: "Recent Success in Raising Ruffed Grouse in Captivity," *Journal of Wildlife Management*, October 1963.
24. Gray, George Robert: *A List of the Genera of Birds*, London, 1840.
25. Gullion, Gordon W.: "Aspen—A Primary Wildlife Habitat Resource," *Orvis News*, October 1977.

26. ———: Forest Manipulation for Ruffed Grouse, *Transactions North American Wildlife and Natural Resources Conference*, 1977.

27. Lahontan, Baron de: *New Voyages to North America*, 2 vols., English Edition, 1703. Reprinted by A. C. McClurg, Chicago, 1905.

28. Leopold, Aldo: *Game Management*, Charles Scribner's Sons, New York, 1933.

29. ———: *A Sand County Almanac*, Oxford University Press, New York, 1949.

30. Linnaeus, Carl: *Systema Naturae*, 1766 edition.

31. Marshall, William H.: *Ruffed Grouse Behavior*, BioScience, February 1965.

32. Moran, Richard, and Walter L. Palmer: "Ruffed Grouse Introduction and Population Trends on Michigan Islands," *Journal of Wildlife Management*, 27 (4), 1963.

33. Nuttall, Thomas: *A Manual of the Ornithology of the United States*, Hilliard & Brown, Cambridge, 1832.

34. Palmer, Walter L.: "Ruffed Grouse Flight Capability Over Water," *Journal of Wildlife Management*, 26 (3), 1962.

35. Palmer, Walter L., and Carl L. Bennett: "Relation of Season Length to Hunting Harvest of Ruffed Grouse," *Journal of Wildlife Management*, 27 (4), 1963.

36. Peterson, O. A.: *Fossils of the Frankstown Cave*, Annals, Carnegie Museum of Pittsburgh, 1926.

37. Ross, Bernard: "List of the Mammals, Birds and Eggs Observed in the McKenzie River District," *Canadian Naturalist and Geologist*, 7 (2), 1862.

38. Sawyer, Edmund, J.: "The Ruffed Grouse with Special Reference to Its Drumming," *Roosevelt Wildlife Bulletin*, 1 (3), 1923.

39. Sheldon, Harold P.: See Connett, E. V.

40. Spiller, Burton L.: *Grouse Feathers*, Derrydale Press, New York, 1935.

41. Smyth, Thomas: "Study of the Food and Feeding Habits of the Ruffed Grouse," Master's thesis, Cornell University, N.Y., 1923.

42. ———: "Studies in the Life History of the Ruffed Grouse," Ph.D. thesis, Cornell University, N.Y. 1925.

43. Vreeland, Frederick K.: "How a Ruffed Grouse Drums," *American Game Protective Association*, Bulletin 7, 1918.

44. Wetmore, Alexander: See Peterson, O. A.

45. ———: "A Checklist of Fossil Birds of North America," *Smithsonian Miscellaneous Collection*, 99 (4), 1940.

46. ———: "How Old Are Our Birds?" *Bird Lore*, September 1936. (Title now changed to *Audubon Magazine*)

47. Wilson, Alexander: *American Ornithology,* Bradford and Inskeep, Philadelphia, 1812.

Additional References

Beverley-Giddings, A. R.: *Frank Forester on Upland Shooting,* William Morrow, New York, 1951.

Chambers, Robert, and Ward M. Sharp, "Movement and Dispersal within a Population of Ruffed Grouse," *Journal of Wildlife Management,* 22 (3), July 1958.

Churchill, Robert: *Churchill's Shotgun Book,* Alfred A. Knopf, New York, 1955.

Cooper, C. A. ("Sibylline"): See Leffingwell, W. B.

Criddle, Norman, "Some Natural Factors Governing the Fluctuations of Grouse In Manitoba," *Canadian Field-Naturalist,* April 1930.

Dalrymple, B. W.: *Complete Guide to Hunting Across North America,* Harper and Row, New York, 1970.

DeLury, Ralph E.: "Sunspots and Living Things," *Transactions of American Game Conference,* 1930.

Edminster, Frank C.: *American Game Birds of Field and Forest,* Charles Scribner's Sons, New York, 1954.

Foster, William H.: *New England Grouse Shooting,* Charles Scribner's Sons, New York, 1942.

Gross, O. A.: "Annual Report Of The New England Ruffed Grouse Investigation," *Proceedings New England Game Conference,* 1930.

Gullion, Gordon W.: "Improvements in Methods of Trapping and Marking Ruffed Grouse," *Journal of Wildlife Management,* 29 (1), 1965.

———: "A Viewpoint Concerning the Significance of Studies of Game Bird Food Habits," *The Condor,* 68 (4), 1966.

———: "The Use of Drumming Behavior in Ruffed Grouse Population Studies," *Journal of Wildlife Management,* 30 (4), October 1966.

———: "Selection and Use of Drumming Sites by Male Ruffed Grouse," *The Auk,* 84 (1), January 1967.

———: "Stopping the Decline and Fall of Ruffed Grouse," *Field and Stream,* December 1970.

———: "You Can Have More Grouse in Your Woods," *Field and Stream,* October 1971. Reprinted in *Orvis News,* August 1972.

———: "Grouse Cycles: Are They Real?" *Minnesota Science,* 29 (3), 1973.

———: *Improving Ruffed Grouse Habitat with Proper Planting,* The Ruffed Grouse Society, Coraopolis, Pennsylvania, 1975.

———: "Maintenance of the Aspen Ecosystem as a Primary Wildlife Habitat," *Proceedings XIII International Congress of Game Biologists,* 1977.

———, Ralph T. King, and William H. Marshall: "Male Ruffed Grouse and Thirty Years of Forest Management on the Cloquet Forest Research Center, Minnesota," *Journal of Forestry,* 60 (9), 1962.

Hall, Henry Marion: *The Ruffed Grouse,* Oxford University Press, New York, 1946.

Hewitt, C. G.: *The Conservation of Wildlife in Canada,* Charles Scribner's Sons, New York, 1921.

Holland, Dan: *The Upland Game Hunters Bible,* Doubleday, Garden City, N.Y., 1961.

Holland, Ray P.: *Shotgunning in the Uplands,* A. S. Barnes and Co., New York, 1944.

Johnsgard, Paul A.: *Grouse and Quails of North America,* University of Nebraska Press, Lincoln, 1973.

King, Ralph T.: "Ruffed Grouse Management," *Journal of Forestry,* 36 (6), 1937.

Knight, John Alden: *The Ruffed Grouse,* Alfred A. Knopf, New York, 1947.

Leffingwell, William B. ed. *Shooting on Upland, Marsh and Stream,* Rand McNally, Chicago, 1890.

Lewis, Elisha J., M.D.: *The American Sportsman,* Lippincott, Gambo and Co., Philadelphia, 1855.

Madson, John: *Ruffed Grouse,* Winchester Press, East Alton, Illinois, 1969.

Marshall, William H., and John J. Kupa: "Development of Radio-Telemetry Techniques for Ruffed Grouse Studies," *Transactions North American Wildlife and Natural Resources Conference,* 1963.

Mayer, Alfred M. ed.: *Sport with Rod and Gun,* Century Co., New York, 1883.

Norris, Charles C., M.D.: *Eastern Upland Shooting,* J. B. Lippincott Company, Philadelphia and New York, 1946.

Palmer, T. S.: "Chronology and Index of the More Important Events in American Game Protection 1776–1911," *Biological Survey Bulletin No. 41.* March 12, 1912, U.S. Department of Agriculture, Washington, D.C., 1912.

Palmer, Walter L.: "Ruffed Grouse Population Studies on Hunted and Unhunted Areas," *Transactions North American Wildlife and Natural Resources Conference,* 1956.

Rich, W. H.: *Feathered Game Of The Northeast,* T. Y. Crowell and Co., New York, 1907.

Sandys, Edwyn, W., and T. S. Van Dyke: *Upland Game Birds,* Macmillan, New York, 1902.

Svoboda, F. J., and G. W. Gullion: "Techniques For Monitoring Ruffed Grouse Food Resources," *The Wildlife Society Bulletin,* 2 (4), Winter 1974.

Tavenor, P. A.: "The Ruffed Grouse And Island Populations," *Canadian Field-Naturalist,* June 1940.

Woolner, Frank: *Grouse And Grouse Gunning,* Crown Publishers, New York, 1970.

Index